First published 2011 by Edinburgh City
Libraries
ISBN 978-1-906401-36-8
Copyright © Dyslexia Scotland
The right of Dyslexia Scotland to be identified
as the editor of this work has been asserted
by them in accordance with the Copyright,
Designs and Patents Act 1988.

Acknowledgements

Dyslexia Scotland would like to extend our sincere thanks to all the contributors of the stories in this book. Some of the contributors are members of Dyslexia Scotland, some heard about the project through our network and others through a variety of sources. We thank you all for your invaluable contributions.

We would also like to extend a special thanks to Tamsin Morrison, an artist with dyslexia who designed the front cover of this book and to our President, Sir Jackie Stewart, for his foreword and for contacting a number of celebrities to ask them to write their stories.

Our deep gratitude goes to Edinburgh City Libraries for funding this book, and in particular to David Walker for publishing it and to Councillor Deirdre Brock, Liz McGettigan and Grainne Crawford for their valued support.

About Dyslexia Scotland

Dyslexia Scotland is a national charity that represents the needs and interests of dyslexic people in Scotland. Our aim is to encourage and enable children, young people and adults with dyslexia, regardless of their age and abilities, to reach their potential in education, employment and life.

We offer high quality services at both a national and local level through our network of volunteer-led branches. We also aim to raise awareness and influence change at a national level.

For more information:
www.dyslexiascotland.org.uk

Dyslexia Scotland
2nd Floor – East Suite
Wallace House
17-21 Maxwell Place
Stirling
FK8 1JU

Office: 01786 446650
Helpline: 0844 800 8484

Dyslexia Scotland is a charitable company limited by

If you have been moved by these stories, please
consider making a donation to Dyslexia Scotland
or joining as a member so that we can continue to
support dyslexic people of all ages and abilities across
Scotland.

Foreword
by Sir Jackie Stewart OBE
President of Dyslexia Scotland

Today, dyslexia is talked about more openly than it ever has been.

When you are dyslexic, you simply cannot do things like "the clever folk". Some say it's a sort of wiring error between the left and the right side of the brain. Others say that it is hereditary, or it is caused by a long labour in birth, or perhaps a jaundice birth. It can sometimes jump generations, but quite often, it shows up within the family tree. Dyslexia can destroy people, it can break up families and it can drive people to drink and drugs whilst they are trying to escape the reality of their inabilities.

For many years and sadly even today, many teachers simply haven't gone to the trouble of finding out enough about dyslexia to help students to get around the problem, if not to get over it completely. My school years were certainly the most unhappy years of my life. Back then, few teachers had any knowledge at all about something called Dyslexia.

What has been achieved by Dyslexia Scotland surpasses anything done elsewhere. The education authorities and the seven teacher-training colleges in Scotland have now, with the help of the present and previous Scottish Governments, turned around the attitude of many of the professional educational leaders in our land. From last year onwards, every single new teacher being trained in any of our seven teacher-training colleges in Scotland will, upon leaving college, be in possession of a degree which includes the skills for the early recognition of a child with a learning problem. No other country in the world has this; what a wonderful example Scotland is, to the other educational leaders around the world.

The question is whether the other educational leaders will pay attention and whether old dogs want to learn new tricks? Sadly, sometimes not. The damage that they do however, by not knowing how to deal with a young person with learning difficulties, is far beyond their comprehension. The parents become mightily distressed; they are told many times in the school reports that their child is not paying attention, is not concentrating, is lazy, not doing their homework, or is even seriously disruptive within their class or school. Many leave school with very few skills for reading, writing or numeracy. I was one of those children, but I had ambitions and I desperately wanted to be good at something. I wanted to make a living and was ambitious about one day affording some of the wonderful things that I could see other people enjoying.

Many young people who leave school are told they are 'unemployable'. Partially because, nowadays, there's a thing called a job application form, which the large majority of dyslexics would never be able to fill in. When they are continuously turned down, because of their lack of skills in reading and writing, quite often they turn to crime as it pays better than unemployment in most cases but, of course, they more often than not end up in prison, at a huge cost to the nation, which disrupts their marriages, their parents and their brothers and sisters. They lose their own confidence and self-esteem and many of them turn to violence in frustration; particularly if they are of tall and heavy build; they simply cannot take it any more and they lash out.

I, myself, have been working with Kenny MacAskill, the Minister of Justice and Mike Russell, the Minister of Education, trying to put pilot schemes together, in Saughton Prison in Edinburgh; the "home" of over 900 detainees. Many of them don't want to admit that they can't read or write, because to their mind, it shows a weakness that could be taken advantage of by other inmates. We have been trying to increase the education for prisoners within the penal system, so that while they are in prison, they could in fact become capable of reading or writing by the time their sentence is served. If that were to happen, we hope they could rejoin society to be productive, support their families, rebuild their lives, become decent parents to a growing family and no longer take up many man-hours from the police force and be disruptive. However, if we don't help them in prison, the chances are that they will become serial detainees.

A lot still has to be done and much has to be learned. It's far from being unilaterally dealt with in the appropriate fashion by government, the local authorities, the educational establishments, the police force and even the armed services. However, if the will is there, we can all perhaps find a new way of doing business by thinking out of the box and by keeping pressure on our government and our educational authorities around our country not to abandon the potential of the people who have been discarded in many cases educationally.

Leonardo da Vinci was dyslexic, as was Albert Einstein, along with some of the wonderful film creators; Steven Spielberg and George Lucas. Some magnificent sports people; Mohammed Ali or Sir Steve Redgrave. The Bankers, such as Charles Schwab of the United States of America, who made a huge fortune by going about his business in a different way, because his dyslexic mind found a new way to direct people to make money by banking with him.

The wonderful examples of the people who have chosen to tell their stories in this book should give every person who has got learning difficulties hope and enthusiasm for the future.

I thank all who have contributed to this publication from the bottom of my heart and passionately plea that more people will do more to achieve a better chance for those who could so easily be damaged, and even lost, by their own frustrations.

Councillor Deidre Brock
Convenor for Culture and Leisure

It is my great pleasure to write on behalf of Edinburgh City Libraries and Information Services about the development of this wonderful book of inspirational stories.

There are many definitions of Dyslexia; however it has traditionally been described as "a continuum of difficulties in learning to read, write and/or spell, which persist despite the provision of appropriate learning opportunities. These difficulties often do not reflect an individual's cognitive abilities and may not be typical of performance in other areas." Dyslexia occurs at all levels of intelligence, average, above average, and highly gifted.

It has been an honour to read these powerful life stories, as I know first hand from the experience of family members how debilitating dyslexia can be. As you begin to read these stories from our guest writers, some of course very well known to us, you will be inspired by their sheer strength and determination. As you continue to read you will see that this is a common theme running through the lives of ALL our storytellers. Some stories will make you laugh, some will make you cry, but every single one allows you to view dyslexia through the eyes of those it affects.

Reading and Learning is at the heart of Edinburgh City Libraries and this book shows how important it is for everyone to understand the obstacles and challenges that our storytellers have to overcome on a daily basis.

I am really delighted that Edinburgh City Libraries were able to work in partnership with Dyslexia Scotland to develop this moving, encouraging and motivational book.

A note to the reader about this book

'Dyslexia and Us' is a collection of over 100 personal stories from people of many different ages and backgrounds about what dyslexia means to them.

Dyslexia Scotland has been overwhelmed by the response we have received from people wishing to share their own reflections and experiences, whether or not they themselves are dyslexic.

This is a collection of moving, poignant, sad, witty, shocking, instructive and illuminating stories. They describe the powerful impact of dyslexia on individuals, families, relationships, professionals and support staff from a fascinating spectrum of different workplaces and day to day situations.

A few points to note:

• Although we have edited some aspects of the stories such as punctuation, we have chosen not to correct spelling or grammar mistakes. We recognise that some people may have found it difficult to write their story and we wanted to hear their stories told from the heart.

• We have also respected the wishes of many of the authors who asked that we do not reveal their identity. We did this by not naming them and by taking out references within the stories that would reveal the identity of the author and those who support them.

• Other authors wanted to be named and we have respected their wishes by including their full names.

• There is no significance in the order in which the stories have been arranged. We deliberately decided not to organise the stories into chapters on different themes, so that readers could browse the stories at random and see the impact of dyslexia across society.

• The Contents pages provide readers wishing to look at specific aspects of dyslexia with the title of the story and the background of its author.

• The stories are personal experiences and opinions and are not necessarily the views of Dyslexia Scotland.

Contents

1. Form-filling and panic
"I had never fild in a form befor starting a job – Panic"

One hearable Winters moring I was out looking for work. At the time their were thousands of constriction workers ether payed off or layed off because of the prolonged freezing conditions. Things were desperate, bills not being payed, Christmas coming on, not a coin to my name. Walking along the road in Govern Glasgow I spotted a mobile concrete mixer entering Einfileds ship yard. Conning my way past the gateman and on to the site. Fortunately I new the general foreman from previous jobs. I asked, "are you starting any men?" "yes" he said. (My hart mist a couple of beats) "Start rightaway, but you must fill in a form befor you start work". I had never fild in a form befor starting a job - Panic –

"Alic could I have an hour the wife is outsaid the gate, I must go and tell her I have to start work rightaway, would it be ok if I start after the dinner brake at one pm?" "Ok", he said. Passing the office on the way out I packed up an application form. Back out on the raod again, unable to read or write and a form to get fild in ten minuets already gon. Panic building up I was seeing doble.

Just across the way a church, making my way

towards it thinking the minister might help me. No, bad ider, along the road a bit a labour exchange, went in, big cueus of unemployed men, no good out again. Next door a ploice station, got to the front desk and took cold feet.

Panic with my head full of broken botels and time tacking away 35 minuets gon. Right in front of me was the famous pierce institute, inside people were having lunch and outhers were serving the meals, the office was closed. The semel of food made me dizzy.

On the street again I was busting for a pie, made for the underground toelets at Goven cross. On the way out I spotted the toilet attendant in his wee office reading a book and thought if he can read he will be able to write and spell. Hesitating then finally knocked on the door thinking I'll just go for it, I was desperate the clock was ticking away 45 minuets gon. "Could you do me a favour please?", "If I can, what is it?" the attenuant said. "I must get this form filed in so as I can start work at one o clock and I cant read or write."

It felt like the blood was draining out of me. "Carm down," he said "it'll be no bother". He asked the approbate questions and fild the form in effortlessly. "do you want me to sign it for you?" "yes" and gave my name. "Thank you, Thank you". On the way out I had a quick look at the from it was lovely writing and the signature mached.

Estimating I had about 9 minuets to get back to the site I ran like hell handed in the form and started work hungry but bang on time.

The job lasted in to May of the following year. At the time I was unaware I was dyslexic. However over the years steady progress has been made all the time speling writing and reading in fact most of my spear time is spent reading.

After retrment I spent some time at College. I ganned some qualifications. We in the class wanted mor but they puled the plug on us. Financial problems.
Brian King, dyslexic retired construction worker

---

2. Having ambitions
"I want to be the best I can be in anything I try"

I am Alexander Orr, I'm 16 and I have dyslexia. My Dad and my uncle Duncan along with my cousins all have dyslexia. My Grandpa didn't write too, but he was a very successful farmer leaving school at 13 and built up to buying seven farms. I want to be a farmer and rally driver, I also would like to play rugby for Scotland.

I hated school and really glad I have left to go to

Oatridge College to study engineering and hope to go to the Scottish Agricultural College to then study farming, engineering and get some help with my IT. I cannot understand why the teachers thought I could read things when I could not and nobody would listen to me. For the first two years of school I stood out in the corridor, but I can't remember why exactly. Children with dyslexia shouldn't be put out in the corridor.

I wish I didn't have dyslexia, but I do and although the school said I didn't have it, they are the stupid ones, not me. When the school said I didn't have dyslexia, and I knew I did, I thought they just wanted rid of me, but some day I will go back and tell them what they did wrong.

I am pleased my Dad has dyslexia as this makes us laugh. I am also co-driver to Des Campbell. We got two trophies in the Jim Clark Rally this year. Des is also dyslexic and we have a really good working relationship, especially in the car. When we are rallying we don't speak to each other, as we cannot handle distractions. We don't understand other teams who are always talking.

I want to be the best I can be in anything I try. I like people saying I am good at things, people with dyslexia should be told they are good at things, not bad. Teachers need to understand, we don't understand

them. There should be a card we can give to the teacher which says "I don't understand."
Alexander Orr, 16 years old

---

3. Dysfunctional or dyslexic
"How many others are there out there suffering in silence"

He was your regular 4 years old looking forward to the prospect of going to school, meeting new friends, learning new things. This was not to be the case, school was an awful experience for my husband, never quite fitting in, considered the class-clown, lazy, stupid, immature - the usual labels a child with Dyslexia is given even today! This was in the 80s, Paul was tested for learning difficulties but Dyslexia was not to be diagnosed. It was official - he was just mischievous and idol, unacademic!

This resulted in Paul leaving school with nothing but bad memories, no qualifications and a world of pain to come. Soon he found himself in the thick of drug addiction and alcoholism, and all the problems associated with that - well why not? He had it confirmed to him all his life he would amount to nothing, so that is exactly what became of him. Do not get me wrong he tried to fit in with society best he could or knew how to, but he always knew he was not the same as everyone else. He became dysfunctional within civil society because our educational system failed him!! It is not coincidence that our prisons are full of Dyslexics - FACT!

It was NO accident that my husband recovered from his addictions after being finally diagnosed with Dyslexia at the grand age of 28, after attempting to become a mature student. A debt of gratitude goes out to the College for their attention to detail that was so poorly missed during his formative years. Finally it was accepted that there WAS something wrong, a mere 24 years after first attending school.

Now you would be forgiven for thinking, well it was a long time ago things have changed and moved on. Not the case! We are currently fighting for our eldest daughter who is now in Primary 5, for the same diagnosis of Dyslexia. We informed the school when she started that there was a hereditary link with her Father, they in turn assuring us there was not a problem and she was a very bright girl. Being tested for learning difficulties in Primary 3 - standard protocol in our educational institute - nothing was flagged up. Why? Because our Educational System does not recognise the need - the URGENT need - for the testing of children who have a known possibility of a learning difficulty or disability passed down genetically by one or both parents, testing for precise conditions.

It has now become apparent that our daughter DOES in fact have learning problems after all - not a surprise to us at all - the school have finally (in Primary 5!) accepted an issue. Currently we are assured she is being tested purely in the first instance for Dyslexia - for this learning difficulty you do need specific testing as the difficulty is so complex and indeed insidious - this is great news you would think, better late than never!

However we now have to focus on the damage that has already been done, you do not suddenly become dyslexic at the age of 9! Our daughter has had to unwittingly, in order to fit in with her classmates and peers, become an expert in finding strategies and putting these in place - I stress unwittingly - in order to fit in and be the same as everyone else, in turn hiding her difficulty to such an extent even she herself does not know there is a problem, let alone her teachers – who, let's face it, are or should be qualified to see exactly that! These strategies have to be positively reversed and used correctly. Even though she knew she was different from everyone else, she does not understand her frustrations and outbursts caused by the lack of diagnosis and indeed failure in her current education. Now thankfully we are being listened to, finally!

How many others are there out there suffering in silence, perhaps ready to leave school considered stupid, ready to join society to become increasingly frustrated because they know they are different and there is something not quite right? Can you imagine the torment? How will they deal with the rest of their life? Will they join the workforce happily likely in a menial capacity due to the fact they cannot fully read, write or calculate, or rebel against a system that has let them down, becoming Dysfunctional!

How many children are there within schools currently AT RISK?

Make no mistake it is - AT RISK - My husband survived his addictions by the grace of God, thus living to tell the tale. This is not dramatic, it is a miracle Paul is alive today. Many many more have perhaps not been so fortunate.

Wife and mother of 9 year old with dyslexia

4. Proud to be dyslexic
"I long ago forgave my form master for the dark days"

I was seven years old when my form master told me that I was stupid.

I was "right eyed" (constantly tried to read from right to left), left handed (not allowed) and slow to comprehend (terrified of being wrong ~ again).

Worst of all I could not spell, just like my father whose letters to me at boarding school were read to me (and critiqued) weekly by my form master.

I only wanted to be like the other boys, but my "afflictions" made me an outcast from the majority of the other 29 of them. I was Goofey Gifford and THICK, THICK, THICK!

All classes, even maths, filed me with dread and English copperplate writing and spelling classes filled me with terror. I would try evey possible conciveable trick not to have my work marked. I once managed to escape this for three weeks by constantly moving to the back of the marking queue. Needless to say, all I achieved by this was a delay in the inevitable anger, humiliation and ridicule from my form master which was then echoed by my brighter class mates at playtime, at meals and in the "dorm". These were dark days, and the sun never shone.

The adults that actually noticed me were the school porter, a tubby, jolly man called Dick and the Religious Knowledge teacher Mrs C..., the wife of a Spitfire pilot killed in the Battle of Britain. They didn't care about my spelling, being right eyed and never forced me to write with my right hand. They saw what I was really good at. I could express myself well verbally, had a great memory for detail and was exceddingly fast at climbing very tall trees. They boosted my self esteem and confidence.

Dick and Mrs C... made me realise that I was different, and that it was something to be proud about, and not to be ashamed or to be defensive because of it. Like me they had never heard of Dyslexia, and it was many years before I was to hear the word, or knew what it meant.

I must have been about 28 years old and on my way with a team to climb Mt Everest (29,035ft), the highest mountain in the world. We achieved the climb successfully putting the 52nd and 53rd climbers on the summit. This was a few years before having my first book published on planning and organising expeditions, which is still recognised as the definitive guide to the subject. Other books and articles have followed as has a life full of adventure and expeditions,

motivational speaking, and various business ventures –
among them as CEO launching Merrell Outdoor footwear
into UK and Europe in 1991, now the biggest footwear
company world wide in the adventure sector.

I long ago forgave my form master for the dark days
he unwittingly created for me. He and his educational
contemporaries were unaware of dyslexia, or any
form of learning difficulties in the 1950s and 60s.
Throughout my education it was never mentioned.
I was constantly bottom of the class, and "thick". I
made school friends out of notoriety ~ i.e. rebelling
and being outrageous when ever possible.

I sometimes wonder what happened to the "bright"
boys that were praised at school for their work. It is as
if they were absorbed into the everyday mundane flow
of the greyness of adult life. I have not seen or heard
of any of them since my teens. And if that's the case,
I'm proud to be dyslexic and to have the alternate
overdeveloped sensory and expressive skills that
compensate for not being part of the norm. They have
served me well, and continue to do so.

**Nigel Gifford, OBE, Frgs. (Fellow of the Royal
Geographical Society) adventurer, explorer,
motivational speaker, author and businessman.**

5. Living with dyslexia
"the way to learning is to find your own way"

Only as I get older do I really understand how my dyslexia affected the way in which I reacted to the class room, to reading and to spelling. My first memory of not being at the same level as my other class mates was in a reading session, I remember looking helplessly up at the teacher for her to reply "why are you looking at me the words are not written on my face." I remember feeling lost with all the words jumping around the page. If it was not for some of the amazing teachers I have been lucky enough to have had, my education would have turned out so very differently. Eventually with their kindness, support, patience and laughter, together we found small solutions I was able to apply on my own. I was so lucky to have found stories such as Harry Potter to inspire my reading and from that moment on I was able to race through books including history books which are my passion. Living with dyslexia for me has been a big adventure, which seemed in the beginning to be something I was going to struggle to overcome. I am so lucky to have it instead enhance my learning in different fields and avenues especially those I have continued to study at university. The most important moment was finally realising the way to learning is to find your own way in the class room and accepting that brain smarts and brightness are not one and the same.

HRH Princess Beatrice of York

---

6. A father and lawyer's tale
"I found the tribunal very stressful despite my profession as a court lawyer"

I am a lawyer and the father of children who are severely dyslexic.

At nursery school my oldest daughter was bright; engaged and full of enthusiasm. It all started in primary 1 trying to do her word recognition homework. She came home with a tin of words to learn. I found the blank expression on her face incomprehensible as I showed her each word and her inability to learn the word or to pronounce its syllables. Each night we had tears and frustration, but never made progress. My daughter became withdrawn and lost her enthusiasm. The elderly primary teacher just said she was lazy; the nursery school teacher said she could not understand. We battled on.

Dyslexia has caused tensions in the family. For example, daughter two (who never had problems reading and writing, but was diagnosed at university as dyslexic by reason of her inability to organise herself) overheard her older sister say proudly that she was now on book 4; daughter two innocently said "I am on book 6" – tantrums and despair followed from the older one. Life has never been easy as all the children were always on the edge with their dyslexia making them so vulnerable to any set back. It took over the family completely and they all got fed up with even hearing the word and the siblings were very aware of the extra demands put upon us by my most severely dyslexic child.

Battling for our children has always been part of our life. For Highers our daughter had readers and scribes and got "As"; but when she moved on to A levels she was told in October that she would not be allowed readers and scribes as her reading comprehension age was 12. Is this a reflection of the standard of A levels? We took the exam board through their appeal and tribunal process eventually winning. That was in April, by which time she had missed the October practicals and the January exams and only managed a "C" without the help she was eventually allowed. I found the tribunal very stressful despite my profession as a court lawyer.

We had similar problems at university. Our oldest

daughter was doing a vocational course. Despite the UCAS Personal statement and the reference saying that she was severely dyslexic, the university had not read this when offering her a place. When she asked for readers and scribes for her first exams the university asked why and on being told that she was dyslexic told her that she could never qualify and would have to leave. We contacted the professional body, who said dyslexia was not a problem. They sent someone to the university to explain that their policy had changed. Meanwhile I was setting up a disability challenge and was in discussions with the Disability Rights Commission to seek funding. The university backed down. Our daughter graduated "with merit".

It was hard enough for my wife and I to battle for our children, and I am a specialist in special needs education law. I know from acting for other parents that it is virtually impossible for ordinary families to battle the system. There is little support to challenge education authorities who do not comply with their obligations to assess and give proper support to children – but then the authorities are not properly funded.

Lawyer and father of dyslexic children

7. A tale from prison
"children should have the right to a full eduction before leving school to give them the chance of a better life or they could end up like me"

I am 38 years old. I am currently a prisoner. I was diagnosed as dyslexic at the age of 8. I have been asked by a freind to try explain the difficulties and struggles a dyslexia suffer has.

I was a happy go lucky child, full of bean hyper to the max. I have spent many a trip to Newcastle General Hospital for being so clumsy. I've had stitches to my head, hands, and legs. The longest period of time in hospital was nearly 4 months after getting a metal pole the length and thickness of a golf club shaft stuck right through the top half of my left leg. This was while I was sledging down a hill in the snow. If it had been a quarter inch to the left I would have bled to death or a inch or two to the right then I would have spent the rest of my life in a wheel chair.

In terms of school it was a no go area from day one. I struggled with the most simple of things in terms of maths, English, reading, spelling as well as writing. I also suffered from memory loss and blurred vision. I now know that this condition is called Irlens

Syndiomae and can effect many dyslexic suffers.
Back in 1981 the every day teatcher did not have the knowledge or the expertise of these conditions so I did not recive the help or support I needed.

Having dyslexia as well as missing out on school due to spending long periods of time in hospatil had a very negative effect on my education and on me as a person.

I hated school becuse I could not grasp the concept of what the Teachers were trying to teach. I was always putting my self down and had the feelings of worthlessness believing that I was thick, stupid. I was so unhappy and ashamed as well as embarrassed. So many feelings all on the shoulders of a young child. 30 years on do I feel the same as I did as a child? And the answer to that is, "Hell yes". I can see now how important education is in everyone's life and instead of getting the extra help and support, I so badly needed I felt I was pushed to the side as well as labled a problem child.

This has reflected on my life over the last 30 years with no GCSE to my name. I left school at 14 full of anger, hate, resentment and frustration. Not a grate way to be starting the next chapter of my life - young adulthood. The burden of not being able to read, write or spell pushes me away from a straight life!

I turned to a life of crime.

I believe this all stemmed from the lack of education as well as being dyslexic as I have a brother and sister who received a full education and have never been in trouble with the Police.

The road to crime and the destructive path it leads you down can destroy you. Isolated in a concrate box with steel door each night cut of from the real world, time ticking away, missing out and losing out on all family events, no more choices to choose until your debt has been paid to society.

I have taken drugs to help rid the feelings of worthlessness and low self esteem for missing out on the most important par of my life. However drugs are not the answer and only leves you with another problem in life to deal with. It can also be a very slippery slope to get off. Drink or drugs are no the answer its addictions that wrap you up and take away all the cares and stresses that you may feel. Only to find them all return the next day that little bit worse. Slipping down the slippery slope to a life of crime hell, misery, hartache and pain.

I have shyed away from eduction most my life becuse of all the negative feeling living under a dark cloud with drawing from the rest of the word. Eduction is the most important thing in life and all children should have the right to a full eduction before leving school to give them the chance of a better life or they could end up like me: being a burdon on the taxpaying people of Scotland.

Locked up in Her Majesty's Prison watching life passing away year after year, time waits for no one and its never to late to learn.

The toughest part is comming forward to ask for the help. That first step will help to chance your life for the better. You can never learn to much or enough in this life.

Dyslexic male, aged 38

---

8. Early recognition triumphs
"we live in a more enlightened society that recognises the condition"

My daughter was diagnosed with dyslexia at the age of six. We had hints that there was always something a bit different in Hannah and indeed we revelled in it ... her creativity, her imagination and her quirkiness were just joyous in our eyes. When her nursery teacher indicated that she thought Hannah was dyslexic (at the age of four) we dismissed it as being unlikely and that Hannah was "just Hannah". However my husband and I as ex-teachers did take the comments seriously and talked it over and monitored what we thought were Hannah's differences to our other daughter and her peers.

We knew she had walked at ten months and was alert and bright, her language had been slow to develop, she became obsessed with certain cartoons and characters and watched them over and over again and could act out entire stories and scenes her memory was amazing. She avoided reading or writing with any real form. She also displayed a reluctance, or an inability, to share as if the common rules of sharing were a threat to her. We later learned that this was a common strategy used by dyslexics in that they develop coping strategies to deflect or avoid the subjects or situations that scared them. For instance Hannah would memorise a story and the pictures with it but could not actually read the words. The delight and approval she received deflected from the fact that she couldn't actually read the letters and words.

Then came the introduction of a new reading scheme (and in my view inadequate training and teaching of the teachers involved), her condition seemed to worsen and reading and writing were becoming very problematic. She was falling behind and we were concerned that this bright artistic child was not coping. Fortunately the school noticed too and called for an assessment from an educational psychologist who did indeed diagnose Hannah with dyslexia. We were obviously concerned and worried about her and much of that was down to our ignorance of the condition and what that would mean for Hannah's education and life in general. I read a great deal to Hannah and her love of books was always evident. The work at school and help she received was making a difference and one of the best days for me was when at the age of around 10/11 she said that she would read the next chapter of Harry Potter on her own! Wonderful to see and now she is an avid reader, novels (especially Twilight), plays, you name it, she reads it.

This has all been achieved thanks to the early recognition that the problem existed, early intervention, smaller groups and intensive teaching for reading and writing in both primary and secondary school (both state schools with a funded programme that links between schools). I can now reveal that Hannah has just passed her Higher English.

However, her condition made me aware of those children and adults that I grew up around who never got that help or even a diagnosis of such a condition. All that talent, all that intelligence was simply abandoned and wasted by an education system that didn't know any better.

In my teacher training and career I had no knowledge of dyslexia ... knew vaguely of its existence but not trained to spot it or what to do if we suspected something was wrong with a child's reading ... again that was over 30 years ago and I know things have changed.

It is much better for all of us that we live in a more enlightened society that recognises the condition and provides educational help. It is also wonderful that so many involved at top levels in sports, the creative arts and prominent business people have been vocal in admitting their own experiences dealing with the condition.

There is still much work to do to help children and adults who have to deal with this condition on a daily basis and a vital role for Dyslexia Scotland to play.

Elaine C. Smith, mother, comedienne and former teacher

---

9. From school to the police force
"Dyslexia does not go away, it still comes to hinder me"

I found out I was dyslexic when I was 30. Before then I struggled at School and in some parts of employment. I was always behind in lessons. I was the boy in class that was branded stupid and bone-idle, getting up and wandering about the class. I hated having to read aloud or having to write on the board, I found it humiliating.

In Maths I was only half way through the Blue book, everyone else was ahead on the Orange book, and by the time I finished the Blue book everyone had moved onto the Purple book. I never learnt my times tables at School and still don't know them. The teacher could only spend a little time with me, as she had to spend time teaching everyone else as they were all at the same stage, I just kept falling behind. I never left school with good grades that would have got me to University. Dyslexia has a great talent for eroding your confidence and self-esteem. I tried hard but always seemed to hit the post every time.

I joined the Police in 2003, I was doing well in the job, dealing with the public dealing with situations, decision-making, problem solving, all parts of the job. But when it came to the paperwork, I hit the ground running, I struggled with it. I lost my confidence, self-esteem and felt very down in myself, loosing my self-belief. I am not ashamed to say there were times it had me in tears with the pain that went with all that. I knew something was amiss and had to change, as I could not keep going on like that. On looking back to my schooling, I thought I might be dyslexic, so I decided to get tested.

The test results showed that I was dyslexic. It was a mixed emotion of both frustration and relief but ultimately it lifted a great weight off my mind and answered a lot of questions from my past. I could now start to work out why I had found learning so difficult over the years and work on how I could best learn now. Of course there was this part of me that felt let down with Schooling having not identified my dyslexia and wondering how much more successful I could have been in learning, but there was no point dwelling on that, it was time to move forward!

Dyslexia does not go away, it still comes to hinder me. I end up in a comfort zone and when I move onto a new challenge of study, it is a challenge and sometimes the dyslexia pain comes back again!

Speak to anyone who is dyslexic, they will all tell you the same things, the struggles they have with it, the pain it caused them, the unhappiness, the tears, the lack of confidence, the lack of self belief, people telling them that they are stupid and thick, not applying for jobs, as they don't think they are good enough. The list goes on and on. You are not alone, learn about your dyslexia, get support and help, you will discover that dyslexia is a great strength. Make it work for you, learn coping strategies and don't listen to the negatives. You will find you are just as gifted, if not more then the 'clever ones'. Look at all the successful and famous dyslexics who have struggled and persevered with their dyslexia and succeeded, you can to.

Gavin Law, policeman

---

10. Extra support should be free
"It is terrible to think how many miss out even now"

As a mother of a son who loved books from the age of a toddler, but found learning to read so hard he would burst into tears when trying to do his homework at 6 years old, I felt desperate for him. Many people would say what a bright little boy he was, but on paper he was anything but and his reading ability was poor.

A cousin noticed him crying, she herself had 4 dyslexic children and she begged us to take him, now seven years old, to an educational psychologist to be assessed. I am afraid that at that time my husband and I thought Dyslexia was an excuse for someone not doing very well at school.

The Educational Psychologist reported that that our 7 year old Jack was very bright, but was suffering from being dyslexic. Fortunately we were able to pay for excellent specialist help for Dyslexics that he then received. Three weeks of "one to one "tuition lifted his reading and spelling age by 18 months and more. It also gave him the confidence that he was not as stupid as he felt in class. We soon realised how wonderful it was that Dyslexics could get help and that their self esteem rose as well as the quality of their work.

The Private Prep School he was meant to go to, accepted him with his dyslexia, and said there was a mother of another dyslexic child, who was doing appropriate training to help dyslexics and she was willing to come in at least twice week. So our son went to the school which had a very academic head master, who could not understand why Jack, who appeared to be bright, was unable to compete with his peer group. He often sat on Jack's bed at bed time trying to help him to read.

On returning to the Educational Psychologist our son proved he was improving but was never the less still far behind his peer group, and would not pass his common entrance, and he pointed out this would prevent him from getting into a good school, and that he would end up at a school where he would be far brighter than most of the pupils and this would cause him not to achieve anything like his full potential. He was adamant that Jack should go to a specialist school, one that helped children with problems such as this, for his last year at Prep school.

Jack then passed into a good public school, and again there was a specialist teacher giving him Dyslexic help and training in study skills, she also supported him when he was playing up with other teachers, some of whom still did not believe in Dyslexia. The Educational Psychologist and the school saw that Jack got extra time in his exams. As parents we were never asked to go to discuss University entrance, and after 5 years Jack amazed himself and us by getting the grades that would enable him to get into a University and came out three years later with a 2.2 degree,

We realized how terrible it was that our son only managed this due to us being able to pay for extra help, and that he was fortunate with a very happy united home, and where he was much loved.

Jack went to a second University in the Far East, and learnt to speak a far eastern language fluently. He spent 4 years helping to start a bank out there, now hugely successful 14 years later, before returning to do an MBA back in the United Kingdom.

He got his MBA and has never looked back and is a happily married family man working in a very varied capacity as a CEO.

I believe that if he had not been very fortunate in his parents being able to afford to get the specialist help for Dyslexics he would never have been able to be educated, and would have ended up a very frustrated person. Jack would have missed out and so would the world have missed out too.

It is terrible to think how many miss out even now; there are many areas that children do not get the specialist help for Dyslexics, or the extra time required in exams. The help that should be out there free for everyone, is not readily available every where in this country even today. Only too often help can be offered, but it is only specialist Dyslexic help that will make the difference along with the extra time in exams.

Mother of adult dyslexic

---

11. A tutor's view
"finding out the ways they could not learn and helping them devise strategies"

I was teaching 4 -7 year olds in a small school (small classes). The learning atmosphere was so conducive to learning and I could not understand why bright, articulate, questioning children sometimes could not learn to read or to write/spell as well as their peers or as their potential indicated. I saw them become frustrated, bewildered by their friends' success when they could not "crack the code" and gradually become disengaged from the process. Their confidence was eroded. They sought excuses – much better not to try and risk failure.

My teacher training (in the '60s) had only introduced dyslexia. I had to follow this up. I took a post-grad course at Moray House and the RSA course on Specific Learning Difficulties (in the '90s). This really opened up a world which had been hidden to me: abounding theories; emotional case histories; amazing research by educational psychologists, neurologists, eye specialists sound therapists – the list goes on. Now this information can be accessed through bodies like the British Dyslexia Association, Patoss, many sites found on the www and, of course, Dyslexia Scotland.

I joined The Scottish Dyslexia Association (forerunner to Dyslexia Scotland) and began to work as a tutor/support teacher. This gave me the chance to work closely with these disenchanted pupils, finding out the ways they could not learn and helping them devise strategies to enable them to work through the maze of symbols to give them control. It was a source of great pleasure to work with these highly individual pupils and engage with their lively brains. It was satisfying to see the pleasure of enlightenment as they acknowledged that small goals gradually brought accomplishment.

There is no denying that school is hard if you find the "3 rs" tricky to process. Much encouragement is required. In a tutoring role, I felt that I could provide a customised spring board to boost not only performance but self-esteem and sometimes a haven for worries to come tumbling out. Through close contact with parents (they know their children best!) I felt that I could bring some understanding and could suggest avenues to follow. Parents were relieved to know that there was a reason for the lack of smooth progression through school and often behavioural issues and appreciated support also.

Many of the children I taught were particularly talented in art, music or creative writing or were spatially gifted and could enjoy success in those areas, while others had keen intuitive skills. I felt that if they could be supported through school, they would contribute a great deal to society. Sometimes I hear that ex-pupils have done just that. It brings a warm glow.

I am glad that, now, there is the awareness and training and practice to guide the children - who learn differently and out of kilter with "the system" - and to help them realise their potential and worth to society.

PS Over the years there have been some hilarious errors which we have all shared with mirth. One Christmas, I received a lovely hand-made card, featuring Santa on the roof shouting out his greeting … except that it looked as if he was about to tumble off as he was shouting out (due to letter reversal) "OH! OH! OH!"

A tutor of children with dyslexia

---

12. A pupil's story
"Sometimes my brain tickles but not every day"

I am 11 years old but will be 12 in January. I have curly blonde hair but my mum straightens it a lot, every day for school. I have a brother, a dog, lots of fish a dad and a mum lots of friends and grandparents and quite a big family. I have just started High School that's been a week now. I think I like High School better than Primary school because you move classrooms and if you don't like the teacher you get to move on. I don't like the English teacher. He said 'write it in your planners' but he didn't say it was for homework so nobody did it. He shouted at every single one of us and he shouted at us and he said if you misbehave you will get ten hits from the whip. He says he has a whip in his house. He says children should be shot and then he started laughing.

Dyslexia is hard because reading and spelling are difficult for me. They were more difficult in the first years of Primary school because I had this teacher called Mrs L... and we didn't do any work. Since then I have been dyslexic. My geography teacher reminds me of her. I got most of the words wrong and I would pause every sentence and I would always ask for spelling but then the teacher got fed up with it. I went to a support teacher at primary she helped me with another group. I still liked school because I found it funny watching the teachers appearance. I was in the lowest reading group and in the second highest spelling group. I couldn't spell that much but I liked the spelling. Maths I didn't like but I like it now because I like the teacher I have now. In primary school my favourite teacher was Mrs S... There was only one male teacher at primary school.

Toe-by-Toe helped me. I am over half way and on page 203. There are 287 pages in the book. I would like to have finished the programme by the end of 2011 so that I don't have to do it in 2012!

My mum and dad organised for me to see someone who would help me. It takes half an hour to get there and every day when I go I see my favourite car a beetle! I keep going to this person who is wonderful so that I don't struggle again. We have a laugh. Play. And that's it! But play games that will learn.

Sometimes my brain tickles but not every day only when I have lots of hard work.

Pupil with dyslexia, 11 years old

---

13. Tears and success
"tears of joy and relief when she qualified"

My oldest daughter is severely dyslexic and looking back on her school days reminds me how unhappy they were for her and the family. She was so frustrated by the teachers and her class mates thinking she was stupid, and consequently she was patronised by her teachers and teased by her class mates. I was either battling with her school to give her the proper support she needed, or comforting her at home, or desperately trying to find alternative things in which she could achieve some self esteem.

I always knew she wasn't stupid so it was a relief when her dyslexia was identified, at least then I had proof of her needs when I went into battle with her school. Eventually we could stand it no longer and she moved schools and it was wonderful when her new school actually read the report from the educational psychologist and acknowledged her high IQ. From then on it was a partnership with her school, as we were on the same side. However, battles continued in the wider world – unable to learn sequences in horse competitions, difficulty in carrying out verbal directions from her driving instructor, and often getting on the wrong bus or train because she was unable to read the notice boards. I persuaded her to ask people near the noticeboard but the first time she did, she got the retort "can't you read?", so she never asked again. There were tears, oh yes, so many tears shed by her and by me as her self esteem was battered day after day, tensions in the family heightened, and I felt helpless.

It was a triumph when she made it to university, a dream that she thought she would never achieve. I cried on the day we took her to university. The university was fantastic in giving her so much support and her fellow students never questioned her intelligence and for the first time she suddenly found herself surrounded by hundreds of friends. Inspired by her success at university, she applied to do a 5 year professional qualification and we held our breath knowing what a struggle it would be for her. However she was accepted on to the course and we continued to comfort, support and encourage her through it and there were tears of joy and relief when she qualified. (Forgive me for not revealing what that qualification is, as there is still a fear of the stigma and lack of understanding of dyslexia that might affect her career).

My daughter's determination has been quite extraordinary, I really marvel at her. She is a fantastic person, she is very outgoing now, accepting of everyone and every situation that comes her way and has a huge circle of friends. I often think that because she has been at the bottom of the pile in despair that she has nothing to loose and just accepts everybody and everything in life looking forwards with an infectious smile. In that sense you could say that dyslexia has made her the wonderful person that she is to-day but it is small comfort for the years of struggling which she has endured.

Mother of young adult dyslexic

14. Unsung hero
"He was a changed man and became much more confident."

Bill was born at Newton of Lathrisk Farm outside Freuchie. He was brought up on various farms in and around Fife area until he was thirteen years old, when he moved to Freuchie. At school he had problems with reading and writing and left at the age of 15.

I first met Bill in 1970 and we were married the following year. In 1983 we were blessed with our daughter Leanne. We did not realise at the time what an important part she was to play in her Dad's life.

I had heard about Dyslexia but did not know anything about it or how it affected the person, therefore I did not realise that this was the reason Bill had difficulty with reading and writing. It was something that he had learned to live with over the years and I just accepted that. I was the one who dealt with the paperwork and he would concentrate on the more practical things. He had many hobbies and was a very keen gardener. He was unable to put his ideas down on paper or explain them very well but he was great at visualising what it would look like.

When Leanne was at primary school she asked her Dad to spell a word but he was unable to do so. After a great deal of thought he decided that it was about time that he did something about it. It took a lot of courage for him to phone Adult Basic Education but it turned out to be one of the best decisions he had ever made in his life.

It was not until 1994 that he was finally diagnosed as being dyslexic which meant that he had difficulty in learning and retaining information. Bill was also diagnosed as having Scotopic Sensitivity Syndrome which altered the way he saw things and kept him from learning to read and write properly. This was the turning point in his life. He was a changed man and became much more confident. When he realised that he had the gift for writing poetry and short stories I was the one who had to type them up and check the spelling. During the time he was writing he started to attend college and eventually became more confident with a computer and was then able to type his own work.

There was just no stopping him now. In 1997 he was runner up in the Fife Council awards, and a few weeks later he was on Scottish Television, Scottish Education Adult Learner of the Year. Then in 1998 he was runner up in the United Kingdom Awards out of 210 entrants. An invitation came from 10 Downing Street to meet the Prime Minster, Tony Blair, to celebrate the United Nations Year of the Older Person. Also in 1999 saw him become an exhibitor in the 20th century museum within the Scottish National Museum Scotland. In the year 2,000 he was Regional winner in the Nationwide Award for Voluntary Endeavour. Then became a finalist in this same award and was invited to the House of Commons where he received £250 in vouchers for himself, and £500 for Dyslexia Scotland. Yes there is more. He was an Unsung Hero in the Sunday Mail Great Scot Awards and received £250 for Dyslexia Scotland. He also attended a Royal Garden Party at Holyrood Palace in 2003.

Bill was a great ambassador for Dyslexia Scotland and regularly visited various groups and organisations to give talks about his life with Dyslexia and how his life had changed at the age of 50. Sadly Bill died suddenly at the age of 66 but I know he encouraged a lot of the people he met to seek help and was an inspiration to many.

June Thomson, Bill's widow

15. Ah'm no' daft after aw
"Just tae hear somebody say these three little words. "YOU'RE NO' DAFT" wiz enough fir me"

You're either stupid or you're a lazy little b*****d the teacher screamed as she grabbed my hair and slammed my face intae the desk.

But ah wizznae stupid.

Ah could tell her aw aboot the different kinds oh birds.

Ah could tell her where they nested an' also what their eggs looked like.

Ah wizznae lazy either, cause ah often helped ma dad when he was away collecting logs for the fire.

Ah also helped tae move aw oor furniture fae wan hoose tae another on the many occasions we got evicted.

Raed it she screamed.

But ah coulnae read it.

Ah wiz terrified. Still, it could have been worse cause she wiz the kindest teacher at oor school.

Imagine if it had been the teacher who brought her dug intae class and would set it on ye' if ye' didnae behave. At 8 years auld ma ankles wid have been chewed right through.

And that wiz how it wiz aw the way through primary school. Ah thought ah wiz daft.

Always in the backward classes. Always left behind.

Seein' aw ma pals at school sailing away ahead of me.

Bue see when it came tae writin'? Ah couldnae be beat.

Ah even won a writin' competition and the very teacher who had slammed ma face intae the desk was sayin' how marvellous I was.

At secondary school it wiz the very same. Hopeless when it came tae sums an' maths an' things like tryin' tae learn French.

Ah certainly wizznae tellin' the teachers aboot the words an' numbers aw dancin' aboot on the page.

Ah wizznae goin' tae tell them that ah couldne remember a single thing they telt me.

Two seconds after they'd telt me.

Everythin' wiz in wan ear an' right oot the other ear as the sayin' goes.

So yet again ah wiz always in the remedial classes. But see when it came tae the auld writin'? Aw the poems ah wrote got pinned up on the classroom wall.

Ah always came first when it came tae writin' stories tae.

One teacher told me he didnae ken where ma stories came fi'. But still ah wiz seein' words like Stornoway as

Strongbow or Narrow as Norway; Concerned pensioners as concrete parishioners. An' lot oh other things. Efter the words stopped dancin' aboot that is.

And so. There wiznae qualifications fir Mr Kelly when he left school.

Oh aye ah got a job down the local paper mill. I left after 15 years. A life sentence.

A kent fine their wiz somethin' else oot there fir me.

But for nearly thirty odd years ah wiz goin' aboot thinkin' ah wiz daft.

Then wan day ah saw a local poet cawd Bill Thomson featured in oor local newspaper.

Bill's poems are framed in many places around aboot the toon.

This article was on aboot how well he'd done despite the fact he was sufferin' fae somethin' cawd Dyslexia.

Ah'd read aboot the racin' driver, Jackie Stewart havin' Dyslexia tae.

So ah made a point of getting' in touch wi' Bill Thomson an' he telt me aw aboot this Dyslexia thing an' ah explained aw the same problems at school etc.

Bill just smiled an' telt me he wiz the very same an' it became very clear from talkin' tae him that he wizznae daft either.

After a lot oh encouragement Bill gave me the number oh Dyslexia Scotland. He urged me tae phone them. Which ah did. The woman on the other end oh the phone wiz askin' me different questions aboot words dancin' aboot an' runnin' along the page when ah wiz readin'. Jist like a train runnin' along a track.

She wiz askin' me aboot memory tae? Rememberin' things. Which for me was a nightmare.

She also asked aboot seein' words an' thinkin' it said somethin' else?

She telt me there wiz thousands upon thousands oh folk like me. An' telt me. No ah wizznae daft. Just tae hear somebody say these three little words. "YOU'RE NO' DAFT" wiz enough fir me.

What a weight lifted from ma shoulders.

As fir leaving the paper mill cause ah kent fine their wiz somethin' else oot there fir me is concerned. Ah had a weekly spot in the poetry section of oor local newspaper.

Ah published various collections oh poetry.

Done a poetry reading at the Embra festival.

Came runner up in a Fife council short story competition.

Wrote and published two novels.

Ah worked as an extra in movies like Braveheart, Rob-Roy, Mrs Brown and Deacon Brodie.

I also became a member of the short lived Scottish stunt school.

The first stage-play I wrote will soon be touring Scotland and Ireland.

I wish, I really wish I could see that teacher who slammed ma face intae the desk aw those years ago. I really wish ah could see her just wan mair time. Just the wance. Cause ah'm sure ye' ken what ah would be tellin' her?

So ladies and gentlemen.

If yourselves or somebody in your family is just a wee bit slow, dinnae label them daft. Dinnae label yoursel' daft either.

There's thousands upon thousands oh folk just like you.

Help is out there if you need it.

I would like to dedicate this wee story to the memory of the poet... Bill Thomson.

Michael Kelly, writer and playwright

---

16. A child's view
"I can't say words right"

I have dyslexia my brain is different. At the unit class it has helping me with my reading because I do my reading every day.

At school I couldn't read and write but I can now.

My next door nadir is my friend is the same as me and he no how I feels. At home my sister and my brother make fun of me because I can't say words right and I get up set and cray.

11 year old boy

---

17. Getting recognition in primary school
"it was finally recognised she needed additional support."

My husband is dyslexic. He wasn't diagnosed until 15, at which point he'd not enjoyed school much, but got through with various coping techniques. He left school at 17 and didn't go onto higher education. But this has not held him back and he now has a very successful job.

We were aware dyslexia is hereditary and so when my daughter started school we were aware to look out for it. From as early as P2 I had my suspicions as the mistakes my daughter made were very similar to my husband. In particular struggling with the endings of words –so not pronouncing the plural or the 'ed' and also similar words e.g who/how, for/of, the/they etc etc. My mum who is a P1 teacher picked up on her

44

reading also, particularly the blending of words and was able to confirm my fears she may have inherited the dyslexia, although my daughter was still too young to tell for sure. She got a dyslexia test at the end of P2 but it was inconclusive.

The two years of P3 and P4 have been a struggle for her. It became more obvious she had a problem during P3. Homework was a real battle. The reading took a long time and the connected worksheet with some written work just ended up in tears and tantrums. More and more we were finding that by after school she was really upset and tearful, which was totally out of character. I was given advice of "you can either have a long fight with the school for support or you pay to go private". I decided to go for the latter and booked an appointment to get private help.

They diagnosed severe Visual Stress and recommended tinted glasses. I was amazed at the test results and the difference the coloured lens made. I was also amazed that the school was not really aware of Visual Stress, use of overlays or anything. The glasses do help but she does have to live with the stigma of wearing green glasses particularly from the boys! Although the Kara Tointon program was excellent for boosting my daughter's confidence as she ended up with similar glasses.

Moving between P3 onto P4 none of the information about her problems and her glasses were passed on. During the 2nd term of P4 I had a meeting with her P4 teacher to tell her the struggles my daughter was having with reading and spelling. Up until then the teacher had been completely unaware and hadn't even noticed. To be fair my daughter did cover it up well and it was only once she was home all the frustrations came out.

After the talk with the P4 teacher school life and homework was greatly improved. My daughter was allowed to use the PC in class instead of writing and I was allowed to scribe her written homework. A great relief to home life. We also learned not to force the reading. We take turns at reading pages, or if she needed to go back to school with the reading unfinished so be it. Over the 4 years she has been at school I feel it is me who has taught her to read what she can and not the school.

Although the P4 teacher seemed understanding there are still things which we find amazing. On the last day of term she made the whole class go through a poetry book, chose their favourite poem in it and read it aloud to the class. Needless to say I got the tears, tantrums and stress at home which my daughter had held in all day.

My daughter got another dyslexia test at the end of P4 and it was finally recognised she needed additional support.

Having just started P5 I am really positive as she has a young teacher who has taken on board all the issues and is very keen for my daughter not to have to do anything that would make her stressed. We found some books particularly useful and my daughter's new teacher has agreed to read them to her class. Even today she came home saying boys in the class were laughing at her spelling, but she knows now to say she has dyslexia. And she can deal with it as she knows she's not stupid and that her Brain just works differently.

Wife and mother of daughter with dyslexia

---

18. Dyslexia identified in adulthood
"It was like a weight had lifted off my shoulders"

It all started when I turned 34 years of age with my manager turning around to me and saying Stuart have you had problems with your reading and writing. At first I was taken aback why my manager had turned around and said you don't seem to be reading your emails properly and you seem to struggle writing and composing your emails. Then I opened up, I've had trouble with all this right through school and at college which I dropped out of.

My manager asked if I ever had been tested for Dyslexia which I hadn't and she said well I'll arrange it for you. So off I went to Edinburgh to be tested for Dyslexia which I was at first dreading but after been tested the person who tested me said "Stuart you do have dyslexia" and then turned around and said "you aren't Stupid, in fact you are very able and with the right support you should go back to college and continue your education". It was like a weight had lifted off my shoulders. I was told at school back in on the Wirral in the 1980s you can't you're not cleaver enough and my parents were told at my age of 11 I wouldn't get an O level so through my dyslexia my confidence was always effected I was always told you CANT. The only one two things I was good at was the sport of cycling and well staying off school as I grow to dislike it.

So two years ago enrolled at Scottish Agricultural College to do a HNC in countryside and Environment Management which was done at distance learning, I also received support in the shape of computer software and study skill support of a person ringing me to see how I was getting on. At first I was really worried in fact my feeling was Stuart this is your last chance, but I couldn't be so wrong the support was excellent and I was made to feel very welcome.

As I finish writing this I now have a HNC in countryside and environmental management but also I was award the SQA local college prize award for the student who has shown the must progression in completion of their award. This has a great affected on my confidence as I know I can do things and also I haven't done badly as a boy who was written off by his school at the age of 11.

Stuart Whittaker, dyslexic, aged 34 years

---

19. The magic of Summer, a film starring Robert Carlisle
"about a man who will never talk about 'how he feels."

It took 25 years before I could find the words to write about dyslexia. Even now there's a sense of embarrassment of drawing attention to it. It's a worry about making a fuss, about being measured against other people in greater need but perhaps above all a burning and lasting sense that it's somehow an excuse for laziness and stupidity.

The words I chose ended up as the script for 'Summer' a film which few will have heard of but which tried to put on screen the experience of a young dyslexic man who liked so many people was never diagnosed and who manifests their frustration in self destruction. Not all film crews form a bond but on the set of Summer there was a kind of will to make it happen. That's partly about the energy and talent of the director and producer but it was striking how many people shared with me a quiet word about how much the story resonated with there own. The film industry was, before becoming dominated by graduates, a place where people could learn a craft and work their way to the top without filling in too many forms. As a result is contains many talented people who, for whatever reason, didn't get on with education.

Summer also forced me to go back to those early experiences and because it was actually shot at the school I went to, to sit in the exact spot where many of those experiences were played out. The little cubby hole where the remedial kids used to sit. The special needs room, and the smell of floor polish and urinals, of school dinners and sweat. There nothing unique about these experiences I suppose. Things like the humiliation of not being able read which Jackie

Stewarts nails so well in his biography. The labels from teachers and children of stupid of lazy and of subnormal. It's a kind of fabric of humiliation which takes along time to unravel, if you ever do. Sometime it's the detail of that fabric that can bring the demons back. While not being able to read or write is one thing not being able to tie your football boot laces is another. It's a small thing but the dread of that moment, of people watching of having to ask someone or tying a granny not. I look back at that boy now and wish I could put my hand on his shoulder and tell him not to worry about it. There's a reason it's the way it is and its not your fault.

I missed a lot of school faking illness and found over the years that its the psychological damage Dyslexia does rather than the practical problems which are the ones you have to watch. I eventually went back to education but whether I did it to learn or to just to prove a point is a still a question I'm asking.

Summer is film about man who has genius for memory, a man who has great capability for love and care and as a result is redeemed. Its also about a man who will never talk about 'how he feels'. I suppose that makes the film harder to watch, not as literary as people might want but there's a kind of truth in those silences that is vital, something which Robert Carlisle's performance of the lead character Shaun so brilliantly captures. The word dyslexic is never mentioned in Summer because Shaun was in the wrong places and wrong class for it to have been an option.

The idea of redemption, of setting the past behind you and living outside box that dyslexia can make for you is still a work in progress for me. The making of Summer and my own path has taught me above all the debt I owe to those who wouldn't give up on me. My family and friends and those who have given me so many second chances made all the differences especially when you run the fine line between progress and self destruction. On the one hand I'm heartened by watching my own son get access to more help but I'm also sadden that such help can still depends on having the money to pay for it. I remain very conscious that there are many Shaun's still out there whose lives are harder and smaller than they need to be because they don't get the help they need.

Hugh Ellis, writer of the film 'Summer'

20. A failing education system
"managing to keep things together despite the wholly negative input from education."

I am writing to you about my son's experiences at school. He is 13 and is dyslexic.

He was very enthusiastic about starting school. It was very clear from P1 that he was having difficulty with his reading. I spoke to the school often about his difficulty at learning. I instigated many meetings with the school because of my concerns about his learning. At the end of P5 he was assessed and is dyslexic. He had already determined that because he found the work so difficult, even though he tried hard, that he was 'stupid'. The teacher he had in P6&7 said to me that she didn't know anything about teaching someone with dyslexia. He continued to struggle and was losing confidence all the time.

When he moved to high school I contacted the school to let them know of my concerns and to establish a positive relationship with the school and let them know that we will support him in his learning.

I contacted the school on many occasions because I realized that he was doing very little work at school and had started to misbehave. At the meetings the school was ineffective and offered no practical support for him and how he was feeling. Very quickly in 2nd year his difficulty with school was making him feel very low. He began to get very angry and frustrated about anything. He started to hurt himself, said he hated his life, hated himself, he wanted to die, and why was his life so bad. He would get angry about something in the house and would throw things, shout, cry, tear magazines, break anything and this would go on for about an hour or sometimes longer. I told the school and the educational psychologist about this and they suggested that my husband and I should go on a 'positive parenting' course which the educational psychologist was running. She (educational psychologist) at this point said that she didn't have a role to play for my son. We went to the doctor to ask if he could be referred to CALMS which he was, however by the time of the appointment my son was in such a distressed state that he refused to go in. At school it was becoming apparent that he was getting into trouble. I wrote to the head teacher making clear my concerns. She said she was "dismayed at my concerns" Shortly after I wrote the letter his report card arrived. He was not on target to pass any of his exams at access 3 level ! He was refused a scribe for his exam. The PE teacher told the class that he didn't like my son.

Things I was told about my son by the school:

- He is lazy

- He's not trying
- I've taught many dyslexic children and they are not like him
- He has a behaviour problem

He began to refuse to go to school. The school said that there was nothing they could do to help as he was not at school. They were blaming us for not being able to get him to school. We were summoned to a meeting with welfare. We received a letter from the social work department saying that the school had referred our son to them and that there were family issues. We spoke to the social worker and she hadn't been told our son was dyslexic. She decided not to visit us as we are supporting him with his difficulties. We sent him to Equine counseling which has helped him a lot with his frustrations. He is starting a new school in August as we have taken him out of his school.

It has been a very difficult time for the whole family, our son also has 3 older sisters, and we are just managing to keep things together despite the wholly negative input from education.

Mother of 13 year old son

21. The value of a tutor's support
"The tutor's mentoring role cannot be underestimated"

Never in my wildest dreams did I imagine that I would become an expert on John Deere tractors! Yet that is precisely what happened when Jacob, aged 8 came to me for lessons. A bright and lively little boy, he had struggled at school due to his dyslexia. As a tutor, I have learned to pick up on nuances of expression and mood and to respond quickly by changing tack in the lesson. Such a change of plan was called for one sunny day, when Jacob arrived and wouldn't settle. I decided to hold his lesson in the garden with all its abundance of visual and sensory stimuli. He spied two rusty lawnmowers covered in undergrowth. Unable to contain his excitement, nothing would do but that we had to drag them out. 'Wouldn't it be fun to give them names and write a book,' I suggested, hoping fervently he would take the bait! It worked and in the writing of his little book which he entitled 'Rusty and Blunt', John Deere tractors were invited to a party! Jacob's passion for machinery enabled us to develop his reading and language skills in an amazing way. It is the flexibility which tutoring affords which is such an advantage when teaching a dyslexic adult or child.

My experiences as a classroom teacher in primary and secondary schools made me aware of the varying abilities and disparate needs and abilities of my pupils. Constraints of time and resources made my task to help those with difficulties very difficult if well nigh impossible. I was only too aware that in the midst of the hustle and bustle of the classroom environment, in which many compete for attention, the dyslexic child could feel 'at sea'. Often a sense of fear, failure and frustration spoiled what should have been a positive, learning experience. For some, stress hormones kicked in, making learning very difficult and sometimes impossible. When I left teaching mainstream education and began to tutor dyslexic children at home, I soon realised that when learning takes place in a more informal environment there are many advantages.

The tutor's mentoring role cannot be underestimated. Parents are relieved to have someone outside home and family who also has an interest in their child's education. A tutor can take time to explain the often difficult technical jargon in reports or might be called upon to visit school with a parent to help make an important decision about a child's education. Adults need mentors too. Assuring them that in fact, they can achieve long held ambitions which once evaded them, with the help of funding and support services which are now available to dyslexics.

Dyslexic adults, who look back in misery at what were supposed to be the happiest days of their lives, may also benefit from an opportunity to learn in an informal environment. They can articulate the pain of wasted years when their true gifts were never acknowledged as they thought of themselves as unintelligent. One personable young father who came to see me confessed that he had become 'a bit of a bully' at school due to his poor academic ability and plummeting self esteem. It was only when he read the story of a famous personality with dyslexia that he came to realise he had similar difficulties. For the sake of his self esteem, his family and future job prospects he contacted Dyslexia Scotland. Assessment brought closure for him. It explained past difficulties and opened the way for him to go forward in confidence, in the knowledge that indeed he had the ability to fulfil his ambitions.

A tutor

22. A talented musician tells her story
"they couldn't understand why I was any good at music because I was useless at everything else."

When I was little I had noticeable problems when learning to do things, which was unlike my big sister who loved reading and still amazes me how fast she can read a book. As well as keeping up with school work in primary school, things like tying my shoe laces, learning to ride a bike, telling the time etc seemed like the hardest things. My parents were concerned with my reading and writing and the teachers said that I was just a little slow and they gave me a little extra help for spelling and maths. When I got to secondary school I didn't get any extra help until my 3rd year, when the school decided I might be better spending more time on English and maths than learning German. This did help a little but I really struggled to keep up and didn't enjoy most subjects because of this. The one thing I did enjoy was music – I started the fiddle when I was 6 and knew that when I left school all I wanted to do was to be a musician.

School was horrible! Some teachers thought since I wasn't good at reading I should practice it by standing in front of the class and reading out loud – which still gives me nightmares! It also resulted in other pupils bullying me. I got asked what I would like to do when I left school and I said that I would like to study Scottish music at the RSAMD (Royal Scottish Academy of Music and Drama) then be a full time musician. They just laughed and told me that I'd work in a shop or something like that as I wasn't clever enough to go to university.

After many years of my parents begging for me to be tested, I found out two weeks before I finished my final year that I was Dyslexic. For me, this was difficult news to take – I'd never heard of dyslexia and didn't know what it meant. Looking back, I wish I had known sooner – I wonder what school would have been like and how much better I could have done.

When I left school I studied an HNC in Traditional Music at North Highland College, I then went on to do a BA Honours Degree in Scottish music at the Royal Scottish Academy of Music and Drama. I met some inspiring tutors at both these places who understood and supported me. My dissertation was really hard work, but with help and a lot of determination (I wanted to prove my school teachers wrong) I managed it and graduated in 2006.

Since then I have worked as a self-employed

musician – performing, composing, touring, teaching promoting gigs and I'm the Artistic Director of the Scots Fiddle Festival which is one of the biggest music festivals in Scotland. I also love photography and have some photography exhibitions.

A couple of years ago I returned to my old secondary school to perform in the Christmas concert which many ex-pupils were taking part in as a surprise for the head of music who was retiring. I was really shocked that one of my old maths teachers turned to a friend who was standing next to me and told them that all the teachers thought I was thick when I was at school and they couldn't understand why I was any good at music because I was useless at everything else.

I really appreciate my family, friends and tutors who have or continue to help me when I struggle with things. Although being dyslexic can be really frustrating that's how I am and these days I'm not ashamed of telling people – I still can't read a clock but now instead of panicking when someone asks me the time, or I ask someone and they say that 'there is a clock up there' I'm just honest and I've found that most people find it interesting rather than judge me.

Eilidh Steel, traditional musician

23. Pressure at work
"it causes tiredness, sore eyes and extreme headaches"

At school I struggled but never got the support I needed. I sat at the back of the class and felt isolated.

When I left school I found it really hard filling in application forms and doing CVs. That meant I did not receive many interviews and when I did get an interview, I was not able to be confident enough to sell myself.

I have to concentrate hard to read things, even leaflets. It causes tiredness, sore eyes and extreme headaches.

I now work as a customer adviser on the phone. Over the years their has been more products available to customers, that meant more reading and writing that is adding more and more pressure at work. There is also a varierty of different systems to learn to use.

I now feel really pressured at work to the point it's all a bit much to cope with. Everything is getting confused and mixed up where I get really tired and have a fear of losing my job which I do enjoy because I was helping the customer to resolve issue or enquiries.

My sister said she goes to a computer class and I thought I would ask her for the number. I phoned up and got an interview with a nice lady who is an Adult Basic Education Tutor. She did a dyslexia test and now I am focusing on progressing with reading writing & spelling.

I have learned about different types of overlays (my study bar) that can be set up on my computer at ABE classes, work and at home. Some thing simple like coloured paper can make a big difference.

I'm still struggling but the classes are helping & making me more confident at work when I am writing & updating customer's details.

Adult learner (ABE - adult basic education)

---

24. A day to remember
"I couldn't stop smiling"

When I was a child my mother, father and grandmother all read me stories which I loved. I was good at remembering them so it was a shock when I had reading problems at school. I still could not read at 12 years old when my father died.

My grand-mother heard about an American school which aimed to help people with Dyslexia, a new word for us! I enrolled for a 4 week, one-to-one course in the newly-opened London branch.

My grand-mother still talks of her amazement

when, after about 2 weeks there, I said 'Ask me to spell constitution, ask me to spell subtraction' and I proceeded to do so and I couldn't stop smiling.

I am now a fully-qualified hairdresser and I enjoy reading books for myself

But I will never forget that day in London when I learned how to unlock words.

Young adult dyslexic

---

25. A hero's journey
"a journey through a dark underworld, fraught with trials and difficulties"

Ding ding, ding ding. My son's mobile phone rang at around 8:30 am. There was then a commotion down the hall so I went to see what was wrong. It seemed that somebody was perpetrating a cruel hoax on my son as they had texted his mobile phone with standard grade results that were way above anything any of us could expect (about 400% above our most optimistic expectations!). It had to be a hoax because the results were not due out until the next day...

As I had been through pre-standard grade revision "hell" with my son only a short time beforehand, during which he seemed not to be able to remember much of what he had been taught, my expectations had been steadily reduced to an all-time low. It was as if he had never been on the course and we were trying to squeeze two years worth of study work into two weeks. Therefore, these results could not be for real! Even when it was announced on the news that some of the results had been released a day early it was still beyond belief and only when we had the certificate in our hands the next day could we bring ourselves to believe it was for real.

My son had been diagnosed as suffering from dysgraphia (difficulties with spelling and handwriting) about seven years previously. Over an eight to ten year period he had also been repeatedly tested for dyslexia at school and the result was always negative. Everybody knew something was amiss but nobody could pin it down. It was not until he was assessed through the good offices of Dyslexia Scotland earlier this year that we found out that he suffers from dyslexia and that it was only his extremely high intelligence that was masking the fact.

I can only say that on reflection almost all of my son's time at school has been a journey through a dark underworld, fraught with trials and difficulties, where there never seemed to be any glimmer of light at the end of the tunnel. In eleven years of schooling I cannot recall even one day in which my son came home basking in the glory of some success, no matter how small. All of this had had the effect of grinding his ambition out of him and leaving him with no confidence in his own abilities and a belief that he was just stupid!

Fortunately, we know a little bit about learning and education, especially that "one size does not fit all". Also I have, and I'm sorry to say this, a healthy scepticism about the primary and secondary educational systems. If I could offer some advice to dyslexics or their parents it would be that dyslexics are as capable as anyone else, it's just that they learn differently that's all! So if one approach is not working you need to try other approaches until you happen upon one that does work. Insanity after all is sometimes described as keeping on doing the same things and expecting a different outcome.

So, what of the future? Well, as of today, my son is the hero of his own story, who has emerged from a very dark place into the sunlight where, for perhaps the first time, he can see his own potential. All of a sudden his seemingly unrealistic childish dreams have been transformed into an optimistic vision of the future. I can't say what the future holds but I can approach it with a new optimism.

Father of son with dyslexia

26. Getting lost
"I got lost changing buses and couldn't put numbers into my phone in the right order"

I am dyslexic. I must always have been dyslexic, but I didn't know till I went to secondary school.

When I was at primary I knew I was different from the other pupils but I didn't know why, so I hid it from everybody. I learned to read and write just like as everybody else in the class but over the years I found it increasingly difficult to keep up, though I didn't have any trouble understanding what was going on in the classroom – except for Maths! My strategy at this stage was to copy from my friends. When this didn't work or when I got really tired, I developed 'headaches' or 'stomach aches' and had to go to the nurse's room to lie down.

By primary year 5, I was very worried and I finally told my mum about my difficulties. She was great and went to talk to my teacher who said that I did have a bit of a problem, but there was nothing to worry about. I thought that my teacher didn't understand but I was quite pleased that she didn't know just how badly I was doing. After a while, I told mum things were OK but actually, they were getting worse.

During my last year at primary I found it harder to copy from people because they worked much faster

– so my spelling got worse and worse. I found that if my writing was messier, the spelling was not so noticeable, so I started to write badly all the time. Even then, the teacher decided I was just more careless and that I wasn't concentrating or trying very hard when doing written work.

Life at secondary school was OK at first. I got on OK with the new people in my class and I could keep up with most of the class work so I didn't fall behind – I just spent hours every night getting Mum's help with doing homework so I was permanently tired. I got lost in the school building if I didn't stick with the class and I didn't dare ask to go to the nurse, because I didn't know how to find the medical room.

After the first term I started to find it harder to understand things in some classes and people were getting fed up with having to keep me right all the time. Some of them thought I was boring because I didn't meet them in town or text them – but I thought that if I told them I got lost changing buses and couldn't put numbers into my phone in the right order they would laugh at me. I think people thought I was stupid because they talked to me less and stopped asking me to go places. Then I felt even more left out because I couldn't join in the talk about doing things after school or at the week-end.

One day a teacher kept me back at the end of

a lesson to lecture me about daydreaming and not paying attention (though I had been) and by the time I got out the rest of the class had gone. I couldn't remember what the next lesson was so I wandered around hoping to find my class until the corridors cleared. Then I hid under the stairs where no-one would see me till the lesson was over. At lunch time the others in my class wanted to know where I had been, so I told them I was sick.

After that, I found it easier just to hide rather than to try to keep up with the class, till eventually I just stopped going to school altogether. I would leave home as usual then wait till mum had left for work and go back – and when the school phoned, I pretended to be mum and said I was ill. I don't know what would have happened if mum hadn't come home unexpectedly one day and caught me – but she did and it all came out. This time she insisted that the school arranged for me to see the educational psychologist who gave me a few tests and told me I had dyslexia.

This didn't mean very much to me at the time – for all I knew I could have had measles – but my year head arranged for me to see the Support for Learning teacher and she explained it to me.

Best of all, she showed me a red line painted on every corridor wall in the school – if I got lost, all I had to do was follow that and I would end up at her door and she would help me find my class.

Finding out what was wrong made a huge difference to my life. The year head did a lesson about dyslexia and showed everyone pictures of lots of famous people who were dyslexic - my class started calling me Jamie after Jamie Oliver and asking me for recipes. Mum put all the class numbers in a mobile phone for me and gave me an emergency taxi fare in case I got lost when I was out. I'm still dyslexic – it doesn't go away – but I feel better about it now.

Pupil, male, aged 15

---

27. Failed by the education system
"five years of fighting for support"

Being the wife and mother of a family of dyslexics is a tough job. Although I knew nothing about dyslexia until a few years ago, I had a fairly good idea my husband struggled with literacy and his explanations of events were often legendary.

Living with dyslexia is a two-way struggle. My husband always told me he was different, he always described it as people in a street, everybody was on one side, he on the other. I didn't quite get it until our son was diagnosed with dyslexia, and it all clicked. Dyslexics are different, but the compensation and coping mechanisms they produce should be seen as a resource, not a hindrance. Non-dyslexics often cause the problems because they have conformed to what is laughingly called "the norm."

Our education system has failed both my husband and our son. Both hated school with a vengeance. It is difficult to motivate teenagers, and we always appreciated the teachers who did manage to extract good work and excitement from Alexander. But after five years of fighting for support, and eventually receiving the first psychologist's report three days after he left school, it did not inspire us to write with great appreciation of the process we had become embroiled in, just to seek a little help for a child who was crying out for support.

It is important to know there are bodies and people out there who can help. Dyslexia Scotland was the key to our survival, and it is important to know that there is someone who understands. It is also important to hear of those who have succeeded, and for those who have overcome the fear factor of dyslexia and become comfortable being who they are, and that there can be a point where you can laugh at the tee shirt marked DESLEXA RULS.

Aileen Orr, wife and mother of dyslexics

28. Reading and left right difficulty
"I was no stranger to humiliation"

Way back in 1951 I was sent to the Army aged 17½, my basic training was a nightmare.

I had difficulty with left and right. When the drill sergeant shouted "right tern" I went left and when he shouted "by the left, about tern" I went of on the right food instead of the left. Consequently bumping in to the rest of the squad coarsing mayhem, the dril sereant went absolutely potty, read-faced vanes sticking out of his neck.

Eventually they marched me of to the guardroom charged with insubordination and flung me into the nick. The gards gave me a real hard time, after about a week they sent me to a military hospital to see a nut doctor. On completion of a number of tests he recommended my discharge.

But their was a problem. The Army could not discharge me because there was no were for me to go so they sent me back to 18 battalion on general dutys, latrines, gardening and whitewashing everything in site. Six months later they put me to a new job, it was a project that was to tarn 3 neson huts into a recreation centare, when they were ready my job was to look after them. The ferst hut was to be the library and a quiet room the next hut a church and the third hut a T.V. room. Within a few weeks the project was up and running except the library had no books. It wasn't long befor the books arrived they were in a dreadful state. I spent a week cleaing dusting the books sorting them out according to size and colour then on to the shelvers, small books on the top shelvers and so on down to big books on the bottom.

I stood back and lit a fag admiring my work, even if I say it myself it looked good, very impressive very Regimental. Coming back and forth looking at my handy work. For the first time I felt good about something that was done by me with out any supervision. The silence was broken by heavy fot steps, the door was fluing open, in came the seregnt major "Coming to attention 22216608 privert KING sir, premises ready for your inspection", he went round the quiet room found a cupule of faults "Get them cleaned up, in to the library and onto the outher huts".

He informed me that the education officers inspection was to be at 11 AM tomorrow, and the official opening the next day at 2 PM. I couldn't sleep that night thinking about the library and if anything was a miss finally convincing my self, everthing was just fine.

The education officer went to the church hut first

then to the T.V. hut on to the third hut. He went round the quiet room, their was a fant smile on his face, the excitement was overwhelming. Finally the officer and his sergeant went into the library they stood looking at the book shelvers for quiet some time.

Then the officer with his kain emptied a row of books on to the floor.

"Seargeant get this lot sortied out befor the opening". I felt unendurable humiliation. It took a while but soon got over it. I was no stranger to humiliation.

The sergeant came back with two Civilian office staf it took them about 4 hours to sort out the library.

As the the sergeant left, one of his stafe gave me a register and a booklet of instructions. It was suggested that I read them carefully. "Sargeant I am unable to read".

As it turned out the only part of the new facilitates that were ever used in my time in charge was the television room it was packed every night.

I know now what non fiction and fiction, biographys and so on. I have read hundreds of them.

Over the years I have tried to improve my education and will continue. If you try hard enough and long enough, in my case most of it stuck. Fifty years later when my confidence allowed I enrolled at College in

Glasgow. Got some qualifications anall.

We wanted mor but they puled the plug on us. Financial problems they said.

PS Finally a wee joke. I must have been the only librarian in the wold who could not read. And the only catholic in Britain in charge of a protestant church. That's the Army for you.

Brian King, dyslexic retired construction worker

---

29. Good help at school
"The school turned out to be great!"

"At the beginning of my 6th year at primary school, I was starting to find it hard to understand in some subjects and I managed to persuade myself that I had a hearing impairment! I had problems following what my science teacher said at the best of times (he had a very funny accent) and one winter day when I had the sniffles it was worse than ever. I asked the person next to me what the teacher had said, but he was behind me and heard – and he asked me if I was deaf – so I said 'Yes'.

Things moved fast after that - my parents were called in and I was taken off to have my ears examined. The tests using the machines at the special unit were a bit more complex that I had bargained for, so my deafness 'miraculously' cleared up.

My parents had been worried about the huge amount of time I spent on homework every night so after my hearing was given the all clear, they arranged for a full assessment of my difficulties.

Within a week I was tested by a psychologist and the results clearly showed that I am dyslexic – I have a very poor short term memory, my reading is inaccurate and my spelling was at the six year old level (its not much better now). But the relief was enormous!

The school turned out to be great! Once my dyslexia was exposed and my difficulties were out in the open, my teachers gave me a lot of help. Apparently my short term memory does not work like a 'normal' person's, so I forget what has just been said to me – it seems to slide right out of head. No wonder I could never find the right page! I had thought that this happened to everyone, but apparently not – most people manage to keep things in mind for as long as they need.

Then it turned out that my teachers had thought that I was just not interested in some subjects or that I couldn't be bothered to take care with my work. If only they knew how long I had labored over what they thought was a careless scribble! They became very helpful, providing me with class notes so I did not have to try to write them myself – the science teacher who had started the whole process actually gave me all the class notes from the start of the year! How I had misjudged the man!

I was offered the chance to attend small group tutorials before school started with the Support for Learning teacher – I hadn't known that was possible. I jumped at the chance (even though it meant getting up an hour earlier), and I soon found myself reading much better using a sheet of coloured plastic to keep the words from moving around (I have tinted specs for that now). When I took my plastic sheet to music, it was miraculous! There were actually individual notes on the lines! Until then I had seen these as black clumps that I had to sort out into the correct notes. Suddenly my sight reading of music improved and my flute playing got a lot better!

I started learning keyboarding so I could use a laptop computer for written work. This was just great! My fingers were actually quite nimble (comes from playing the flute, I suspect) so I found keyboarding quite easy and I was soon pounding away at a computer keyboard, producing pages and pages of writing. It was so great – no longer would I spend hours painstakingly creating handwritten pieces – the shorter the better. Now I could write as fully as I speak – and nearly as fast. The spelling was atrocious and my heart sank when I read my first printed piece – it looked great – neat, clean and so professional – till you tried to understand it. But joy of joys! The computer had software to check my spelling, so the next version was much better.

Best of all – when there is a test, I get to do it in private with my trusty laptop and a learning assistant or teacher who will help with the reading to make sure I don't miss out any words or misunderstand the questions. Some even help with the spell checking of my writing – though none of them will tell me any answers.

I used to think that I would end up dropping out of school and end up stacking shelves in some supermarket – but no more. Learning that I have dyslexia has given me a whole new view of life, and I now know that I can have the same ambitions as anyone else – I may just have to take a different route to get there.

Pupil, female, aged 14

30. Memory problems
"memory's the worse part of my dyslexia"

I work in a nursery and as a nanny I found I had Dyslexia 4 years ago. up till then I'd no idea.

One of the things I find hard about having dyslexia is memory.

I have both short and long term memory problems which means I sometimes forget things I've just done I also sometimes forget things I've just done in the past such as holidays, childhood and school.

I work in a nursery 2 days a week and have to remember names. This I find very difficult especially if I'm stressed I overcome this by asking other members of staff the kids' names or looking up at the place where we keep nappies as their names are written on this. I look at the names then eventually put a name to the face by alimenting the other ones.

It's harder when they move to the next rooms as I'll meet them on the stairs and my mind will go blank. I once met a child I looked after for 10 years and couldn't remember her name as she was in a place I didn't expect to see her.

I work better if things go in order at about the same time each day or the same time of the week for example 8.30 breakfast at nursery or Tuesday for the toy library when I'm nannying.

I went on a memory course to see if this would help but it was too academic for me.

I'm now doing a psychology course at night school. Which I find more intreasting. Eventully I'm hoping to find out how my mind works and why it works different to other peoples.

I find it hard to take instruction and take telephone calls as I forget what's been said unless I write it down straight away.

I go away by myself on single, walking coach holidays and if I concentrate really hard. I don't get too lost or miss the coach. I do this by writing down.

Pointers in a notebook such as times we've to be back, street names ect ect.

If somewheres really confusing I go round with someone else. Though I don't like doing this as I feel I'm failing somehow.

I also have trouble remembering words which makes it hard to make friends as I can't always think what to say or rember whats been said. So quite a lot of the time I stay quiet so I don't appear stupid.

As I said I think memory's the worse part of my dyslexia. Though I have other traits such as spelling, left right, directions and numbers ect ect.

But on the whole I manage to get around most

problems and have acieved most things I've set out to do including passing my driving test, passing exams at school not very well but enough to get me whire I am today which is working with kids. I'm also doing night school courses which may lead to further education. This I thought I wouldn't be able to do as I've always been treated as though I was thick and wouldn't be able to cope.

So Dyslexia has both good and bad bits. I think it makes you more determined to push yourself and prove yourself while other non dyslexics give up.

Nursery nurse

---

31. Dyslexic difficulties
"Riteing and copeying are hard."

I have diflculty to reed and rite.

Dyslexia is a problim wen the brane wurccs difurently. I trid my best but I got pict on cus I cood not spel my name till P4. I trille my best but I can't reemember things, exspeshaly spelings. Riteing and copeying are hard.

10 year old boy

---

32. Lost potential
"I am still saddened about what could have been"

When I was a primary school child I never got great reports, OK but not great. Some teachers said I was not trying. I used to be sent out to look after the cacti/plants when lessons were going on to try and give me something to do. Why then when any questions were asked in the class was my hand always the first up with the answer and that I new all the cacti Latin names, where they originated from, requirements etc. there seemed a huge imbalance and yes I was a nerd! Even at high school I was considered immature and lacking in some way. I was given an English exam in 3rd year and given 3 out of 25, what does that say to a 14 year old, don't try because even a 50% pass is way out of your league, how unmotivating. Luckily I got a new teacher, Mrs. Spiers, she was brilliant seemed to understand the difference between ability and effort and was hugely motivating. Even though Dyslexia was never discussed the fact that she listened, supported and encouraged me gave me the ability to pass my higher. Another teacher laughed when I said I would like to do Higher Chemistry. I did it anyway and got a B. On hearing this he shook my hand vigorously and asked how on earth had I done it. I may have smiled politely but I assure you I was thinking something else. It was the same as primary, in class I knew the answers verbally so why did he think I couldn't pass a test.

I came out of high school with 4 highers and CSYS's and decided to go to university. I have always had a great love of the sciences but found it really hard to keep up with the reading. I had thought about my difficulties being Dyslexia and contacted a Dyslexia Assoc. and organised a testing. On testing it was obvious that I was Dyslexic and I was really relieved that I had found a reason for my difficulties. I was given funding for a laptop offered a scribe and extra time in exams. Unfortunately I didn't know how to use a laptop then nor did I have the practice of using a scribe but I passed all my exams with flying colours. Second year was a different matter I really could not keep up with the reading (even with my new pink lenses) and I was getting discouraging remarks from one of my lecturers and he refused to mark one of my papers because the grammar/spelling was not good enough. I had had enough. I was so tired of it all and deeply upset and with much sadness I decided to take a year out which turned into never going back as my confidence was lost. Trying to educate myself had been one long one sided battle and it had had a huge impact on my health and confidence.

Once out of education I got a job in the research environment as a Technician and I loved it. I was learning new things in a hands on way as well as using what I had learned at university. It was the best job in the world (for me anyway!). I am still saddened about what could have been and the thought of trying to finish my degree fills me with dread but I have found people out there who have the ability to understand, help and instill confidence in others. I have since had my own children and my son is Dyslexic. I have so far been pleased with the support that he has been offered and although there will always be room for improvement (there has been a couple of hiccups) he seems to be extremely motivated and thriving. Anyway with a Mum who has experienced the joys of the ill-informed with their demotivating tactics when it comes to education he has a good allie.

Adult dyslexic and mother of dyslexic

33. "The thick one"
"I finally stopped trying to please my parents"

All of my life I've been known as the thick one by my parents. As a child I had trouble with left, right, tying laces, telling the time, time's tables and alphabetical order. I found writing thank you letters an enormous deal. They had to be redone on numerous occasions and often they were not long enough. This was coupled with comments that my younger sisters could write twice as much, make them interesting and be written neatly in a quarter of the time it took me . I remember having to tell the time every time I passed a clock. Also when going to a different room. My laces often came undone which meant that everyone was held up while I tied them up again very slowly. Often I was left behind and had to catch them up.

One evening I clearly remember was listening to a conversation between my parents. My mother saying that she was sick and tired of telling everyone that her thickest child was the oldest .She was wondering would it be possible to change the birth certificates as my younger sister looked older than me and she was so much brighter.

My spelling was poor and I never got full marks.

One word that caused great embarrassment was the name of our road. No help was given learning to spell it. However plenty of comments were made about how useless I was at twelve years old because I still couldn't write my address. It was then I decided that if I remembered a letter every time I passed the road sign on the way to school and repeated them over and over again I could learn to spell the name of my road. This event went unnoticed by my parents.

During my second year at secondary school I was asked to redo a test. I didn't mind as it was one of the few tests that I enjoyed doing. This involved matching and sorting pictures (I think that it was an IQ test). After this I was moved from class 7 which was nearly the bottom class to class 3 with the understanding that I might be in class 2 for some subjects which was nearly the top class.

When I took my CSE results home I was very pleased with myself as I had some As and Bs. However these were ignored by my parents and I was made to feel very small because I also had a D and E. My parents focused on the poor results saying this was unacceptable. This scenario was to be repeated over and over again. It was after this that I finally stopped trying to please my parents. I decided that I was going to succeed in order to benefit my sense of wellbeing. When I was in my 40's I obtained my B.Ed with a 2.2 Hons (this was a greater achievement than my sister had managed). That Christmas old family friends visited and said how pleased they were for me. My parents said that it wasn't a proper B.Ed. unlike my younger sister's. Their friends being teachers said yes it was. However my parents still could not accept this saying that the only reason I could have got it was because the standards had fallen greatly. They knew standards had dropped because the poor state of education was always on the news and they felt sorry for any child I taught. Everyone was rather quiet for a while until their friends told me that they were proud of me. They felt that I had a made a great achievement, particularly as I was bringing up my two girls on my own as well.

My parents only once acknowledged my dyslexia and that was while I was doing an Access course to get into teacher training. One of the tutors suggested I did a test for dyslexia, which I did. When I told my parents that I was dyslexic the reply was yes we know because your school told us. However my parents chose to ignore it and also told the school to ignore it. However they did get me a computer to help me do my degree with the comment, now that you have this it will be the last we hear of this.

Now that I'm in my late 50's I've just done a course on hidden dyslexia which has given me a lot of insight into my dyslexia as well as looking for it in the children I work with. I hope soon to be able to offer tutoring to children with dyslexia.

Adult dyslexic

---

34. Facing up to dyslexia
"Sport became a huge part of my life"

It has never felt overly comfortable for me to talk about my dyslexia. Two of my three children are dyslexic and I am happy to talk about them and how they have learnt to cope using different strategies and they are both achieving at a very high level at school. The classroom was never an easy place for me to be in. I was good at woodwork but then I didn't have to write very much. My strategy was mainly avoidance and when my English Teacher asked me if I would like to come down to the river during lesson time and try out rowing I nearly bit his hand off! I was always reasonably good at sport at school so that can get you around some obstacles. I was also quite a shy boy so I could slip into a seat at the back of a classroom and go relatively unnoticed. I was never given the option to improve my situation.

I was often dumped in the bottom set where I was unable to improve. There was little talk about learning difficulties when I was young and growing up through school like there is today. They often just labelled you 'not very bright' and left it at that. Sport became a huge part of my life from when I was 14 onwards and helped to build my confidence in a different way - just because you have dyslexia doesn't mean you can't achieve – that sort of thing. I still avoided writing and reading and only as an adult have finally come to terms with my issues – of course a personal assistant has helped somewhat! I believe it is so important to identify children at an early age who are having difficulty. My daughter is severely dyslexic but an early diagnosis has meant she is now a prolific reader and writer and enjoys both, whereas I have never.

Sir Steve Redgrave, 5 times Olympic Gold Medallist

---

35. Life with dyslexia: read between the lines
"I experienced great cruelty in the playground."

I don't remember much about school which is probably a very good thing!

- There's not much evidence that dyslexia affects long-term memory but there is strong evidence that humans repress traumatic memories.

My childhood was spent trying to shake-off feelings of guilt and being stupid.

- Weaknesses in processing and remembering new information are key features of dyslexia. These often show-up as blank or confused facial expressions and forgetting what's already been explained, or requested. People generally interpret this as not trying, not caring, or not intelligent and they can feel let down, angry, or feel that they have wasted their time. Many hurtful looks, words and actions can lead a dyslexic to feel it is their fault, and feel they are worthless.

I remember feeling 'odd', misunderstood, frustrated and very, very sad.

- Dyslexia is recognised by a pattern of abilities that has large differences between strengths and weaknesses in predictable areas. This is unusual. People who don't fit expectations experience barriers and discrimination on a daily basis. Expectations in society are based on the usual.

In spite of my enormous effort to impress teachers

and other pupils, my teachers thought I wasn't making an effort and I experienced great cruelty in the playground.

• Humans are social animals, we need to feel we are accepted and belong to a group. We create in-groups and out-groups. Difference presents an evolutionary threat to survival that can override our human compassion. At a basic level fear of the unknown or misunderstood stimulates rejection and aggression. In 'civilised' society people are uncomfortable with acknowledging animal instinct and in order to protect themselves they justify their behaviour by blaming others.

My parents thought I had good potential before I went to school. I could sort out a mixed bag of complicated jigsaws with great determination and I could "talk for Scotland." Pre-school I was a happy wee person, full of life and curiosity for life.

• Although dyslexia can cause delayed and different language development and co-ordination problems, the classic signs of having a vocabulary beyond age expectation, problem solving curiosity and visual reasoning strength can be clear long before children reach school age.

During my school years my parents' expectations dropped very dramatically. Influenced by my teachers, my parents 'laid down the law' at first but over time they decided that they 'couldn't get through' to me. No-one had faith in my abilities, least of all me!

• We understand ourselves through other people's reaction to us. Our self-worth and our views of our own potential are filtered through the information feedback we receive.

High school was a 'sink or swim' experience; the waters were treacherous and since they demanded particular swimming skills, I sunk. I left school gladly, at 16, with one arithmetic O' level; my defence was "I'm not academic."

• Many children with dyslexia enter secondary education without the skills to achieve their potential, indeed they don't know what their potential is. This is not because of a weakness within them but because of a weakness in education, difference is not yet celebrated and value is measured in time keeping, memory, listening and reading and writing.

Discovering my own and my son's dyslexia, a decade later, changed my life. I started to learn. I learned to read and spell effectively through home educating my son. I learned lots about: dyslexia, children's continuing distress in schools, the lack of dyslexia training for teachers, the difficulty parents have being heard, starting support groups (three so far), teacher frustration before they understand and teacher upset afterwards (usually feeling they've let students down), the high incidence of dyslexia in prisons, and the discrimination against adults in the workplace, colleges and universities. I learned how to learn. I passed lots of modules at first then set my sights higher. I now have an HNC in Child Care and Education, a good honours degree in psychology, a teaching qualification, two separate dyslexia specialist teacher qualifications and today I posted my last assignment for a Masters in Education (with equality and diversity), having achieved distinction in the previous year of my course. I have two of my previous tutors encouraging me on to achieve a doctorate.

Clearly I am academic, but that's not what makes me valuable as a person. I have learned that human compassion above all things makes us valuable. How did I learn that? At school!

- Many people learn what is not taught.

Linda Kerr, Dyslexia Specialist Teacher, Diagnostic Assessor, Training Provider and Consultant

36. Educated in prison
"I ended up in prison because I couldn't fill forms in properly"

I was brought up in Liverpool and went to school in Crosby.

This was a terrible experience which I hated and dreaded going every day.

The teachers thought I was thick and needed to go to a Special Needs School. My parents complained to the Council Education Department who didn't do anything, but my parents paid for me to get tested for Dyslexia. When I found out I had Dyslexia and wasn't stupid like the teachers were saying, I was very happy.

In secondary school I was promised more help with this and there would be someone to work with. However this was not the case and a teacher took my blue glasses off me and said that there was no such thing as Dyslexia and they made me read out in front of the whole class. This meant that all the kids laughed at me.

At exam time I was told it would cost too much to put the exams on the computer. My choice was to leave or to stay on as an unpaid caretaker.

After school I started as apprentice plasterer but was paid off due to lack of work. I did a variety of jobs until my accident in 2002 which left me on Sickness Benefit.

Later on at a reassessment I was posted forms that I could not read, so I went to the Jobcentre to ask for help to fill in the forms. They said "we are busy now but come back tomorrow". The next day they said they were busy throughout the day although I waited there. At the end of the day I was told the forms had to be in by the next day, so I tried to fill them in myself. Two days later I got a letter saying they couldn't understand the forms and I was struck off Sickness Benefit.

This left me with very little money and I was due to have my son at the weekend. I was approached by a "mate" who offered me a chance to make some money by taking a bag to Scotland. I was caught by the Police and given a four and a half year prison sentence.

I ended up in Prison where I said I had dyslexia and started going to City Literacy and Numeracy (CLAN) which was 1:1 support.

It was like the brick wall was down and I was getting help at last. A weight was taken off my shoulders and I started writing my story. I also started writing to Sir Jackie Stewart after reading his book about what it was like for him in his childhood. I wanted to say to him that nothing had changed from his time at school to my time, there are still big problems even today.

I also wrote to the Scottish Government and Sir Jackie

about the funding being removed for City Literacy and Numeracy (CLAN) that I had found so useful. After some time this funding has been found and literacy support is still available in the prison.

I moved to the Open Estate and then on to another Prison.

Here I got from one of the warders and I started going to the Big Plus. This boosted my confidence, helped with reading and I learned how to do e-mails and surf the internet. The support I got was not like what teachers had given me in the past and I got more attention, they listened to what I wanted to learn and how I wanted to learn it.

Over the last 2 years I have learned more than I learned in all my school years by getting the right help. The Prison helped me to get the right coloured spectacles which now means I can read books, letters and papers much easier than before.

Because of this I can learn more, access jobs and contact people and services better.

I ended up in prison because I couldn't fill forms in properly and now I feel much more confident doing this. I am looking forward to getting a job and working, showing people that you can get on if you have Dyslexia and how it is important not to put yourself down.

Adult prisoner

37. Good to be different
"We are a good people and have gifts greater than most"

Looking back is always a bit of a journey but here goes.

You can't see it but it is there every day, it is not always easy, but how it is dealt with can change your life.

I always felt I was no good at anything and nobody cared enough to do anything to help me. I wanted to learn, I like learning, but I learn in a different way than most people. People get frustrated and inpatient with you because you don't get it, this is not because we don't have the ability to learn it is because the way they tell it. We are highly sensitive and emotional, we feel that it is always our fault, we are easily led because we think that we are wrong and don't fit in, we are punished because we feel that we must be stupid.

But we are not. We are a good people and have gifts greater than most, we just need a chance to shine. You need to understand our language and we need to find people like us as we understand each other.

I didn't find out until I was 30 years old that I was dyslexic, so it has taken me a long time to realise I wasn't mad or wrong or too sensitive or too emotional or stupid. Just different and that is great.

Nicola Jane Edwards, farmer, winner of the Educational Supporter of the Year category at the Scottish Education Awards

---

38. Life with dyslexia
"can affect almost every aspect of your daily living."

In primary school days, I was in a class of about 25. I found it was just far too noisy to take anything in when the teacher spoke. It was only when it was written down on the blackboard that I learned something although it often took me a while to read it. So I was not so good at school because I missed half of what was said. It's hard to know how much I was affected by dyslexia because I had a slight hearing difficulty as well.

When I got older and started working, I deliberately stayed away from jobs which involved any kind of writing so I went into the building trade and learned a lot of practical skills from older men. I learned how things were done and could soon lay slabs and kerbs in no time.

I soon learned how to fend off those who tried to

ridicule me too. At the age of 20, I became a ganger and I learned how to shout at men so they would do as they were told. When I shouted, people just looked at me and said nothing. I saw the fear in them. I liked that because I knew they would leave me alone to get on with my job.

The lack of concentration and frustration that comes with dyslexia can not only affect your ability to read and write, it can have an affect on your private life. It isn't always easy to mix with others because you lose interest too quickly or can't keep up the effort of concentrating. I often wonder if this lack of concentration and apparent disinterest was a factor in my failed marriage. So, you see dyslexia works in many different ways and can affect almost every aspect of your daily living.

Adult dyslexic

---

39. My son's story (part 1 written in 1985)
"a very unhappy, uncommunicative and at times disruptive little boy"

I have a dyslexic son and daughter and I recently came across the following notes for a talk I was asked to give in 1985 about my son Derek, then aged 9.

"Our son was a contented baby who became an active and often unpredictable toddler. He was fun loving but didn't consider the consequences of his actions and easily reached what I casually called his 'non thinking stage'. He was confident and keen to go to school so while many of the mums were suffering the agony of leaving an unhappy child Derek happily waved goodbye. However, despite the positive start to his school life he experienced great difficulty in learning to read and write. The Infant Department staff worked hard with him and he did begin to read reasonably well although writing was still a major problem.

As Derek progressed through school his difficulties increased. Learning tables drove us to distraction. He couldn't copy his spelling words correctly far less reproduce them. He was always in trouble for not bringing home the correct books for homework and time meant absolutely nothing to Derek. We began to encounter such phrases as "he's immature", "he's very slow", "he's very lazy", "he needs a firmer hand" or "you're overanxious" and "he'll come on". However, Derek did not come on.

While I was concerned about Derek's lack of progress I was even more concerned about his attitude and behaviour. During his P5 year he "opted out". A dramatic phrase to use about an 8 year old boy but it was true. Even when I got him out the door he sometimes lay down on the path refusing to go to school. Eventually he was admitted to hospital and the Doctors diagnosed his illness as psychosomatic. As if to confirm the diagnosis when we went to bring him home from hospital he ran and hid. I don't think I have to go into detail about the soul searching his dad and I did at that time. He was a very unhappy, uncommunicative and at times disruptive little boy.

After a full assessment at the hospital we were told that Derek was NOT slow or lazy but a bright though frustrated little boy. He had a high IQ but he had problems with motor visual co-ordination. It seemed that even writing his own name required an excessive amount of concentration but he wanted it to be perfect. At that point I thought the school would know how to help him but he was in a REPEAT P6 year and still failing badly.

I vividly remember hearing a talk about Dyslexia and the jigsaw pieces started to fit. Jackie Stewart had arranged for the Dyslexia Institute to open in Glasgow and we had Derek assessed. It was actually a relief to us and to him to at last know what we were dealing with. We agreed that Derek should attend the Institute for 2 one hour sessions per week.

We were shocked to receive a letter from the Director of Education for the Council stating that it was illegal to remove Derek from school for the 2 sessions. Many letters were exchanged between us, the school, the Division, the local authority, Child Guidance, our Local Regional Councillor and our MP. While this was happening Derek was following a multi-sensory course at the Institute and was experiencing success. He took off like a rocket! His confidence increased and he began to progress over the range of school activities.

Of course we know that there will still be many difficult times ahead. Derek still has 'off days' when everything goes wrong. He knows that he is dyslexic but he also knows he can achieve and we know that it is not our "fault". There is no sudden 'cure' but there is certainly HOPE."

To be continued in next story...

Elizabeth Dickson, mother of child with dyslexia

40. My son's story continued 26 years later (part 2 written 2011)
"I...wondered what would become of our little boy"

It is amazing to think it was 26 years ago I prepared the notes for the short talk about our son Derek. At that time, if I'm honest, when I read or heard stories of dyslexic children making good progress and achieving success my first thought tended to be that the child couldn't be as badly dyslexic as Derek or my daughter Johanne. Nonetheless I am going to update you on Derek and, yes, it is a success story.

Derek continued to progress in secondary school and, in fact, was a relatively easy teenager to live with. Ironically the amount of hard work he had put in at the Institute had improved his writing and spelling to such an extent that initially the school still argued he couldn't be dyslexic as he was making reasonable progress. However, the Head of the English Department phoned me one evening to say Derek had given a talk which had amazed her and I actually cried with relief to have someone accept that, as with many dyslexics, making average progress is not actually showing the child's true ability so alternative methods of assessment must be used.

Derek completed his standard grades but then left school. He did go to college for Sports Therapy and got a good job as a fitness instructor. However, he got restless and wanted more qualifications but another attempt at college wasn't successful and over the next decade Derek moved from job to job. I lost count of the number and variety of jobs he worked at but he was certainly not 'work shy' and always had a job.

In his mid 20s, encouraged by his then girlfriend, now wife, Derek applied as a mature student to the University to do marketing. All went fine till the first set of exams. He probably didn't even get half way through the questions. He knew immediately he had failed but thankfully his tutor, who knew his ability, later called him in and asked what had happened. Derek explained that he when he was younger he had been told he was dyslexic so another psychological assessment was arranged. Of course, this again confirmed dyslexia and this time the University quickly made special arrangements. He was given computer equipment and supplied with a reader/scribe when necessary. At this more mature stage Derek was confident enough to accept help and you can imagine how proud we all were to watch Derek, our little boy who had failed so badly in Primary School, GRADUATE from University with a Degree in Marketing.

Derek has now been with the same Company for several years. He loves his job and is progressing really well. He is happily married with a little boy of nearly 4. Sometimes I remember the nights I looked over him sleeping and wondered what would become of our little boy.

It is good that more well known, very successful dyslexic people are now openly telling their stories because recognition and correct education should ensure that success can be achieved without the kind of struggle so many children like mine have had to endure. I believe it is true that many famous have 'made it' because they are dyslexic and not in spite of their dyslexia. Maybe one day later in the 21st Century it will be considered a gift to be dyslexic so please remember there is light at the end of the tunnel!

Elizabeth Dickson, mother of adult with dyslexia

---

41. Learning to feel good about myself
"I decided to clear my life of all the things that make life so unhappy"

When I was a child I had so many dreams of what I would be in life; a prima ballerina, a vet, a show jumper and even a policewoman. I never thought I would really be able to do anything well as I thought I was THICK. I had so many difficulties. I couldn't spell properly, maths was a nightmare, I was clumsy and felt so ugly. All these things made for a very nervous child. School was where I went to have all these things confirmed.

Things at school were never easy as most of the teachers had preconceptions and would judge me. I was always very chatty and always getting rows – the same for daydreaming and looking out the window. I remember being made to stand in the corner facing the wall for ages sometimes.

If I struggled with anything the teacher seemed to ignore me or say I should have been listening. The one thing I did get praise for was my interest in history. I got good feedback for my art work at secondary and some of it was sent to Stirling University for exhibition.

It was always the more able children who got to do the fun exciting things e.g. act out scenarios like historical significance. This was normal as I grew to expect it; it was just the way it was. Ironically I was excellent at pop quizzes – to good, so I wasn't allowed to take part in a team so I had to be the quiz master. Can you believe that, something I was good at and they wouldn't let me compete?

I left school with no qualifications and I worked

in factories for years. I hated the job but made some good friends. After finally leaving my partner who brought me down so much I decided to clear my life of all the things that make life so unhappy. I got accepted into college and had the great pleasure in leaving the factory.

I loved my time at college. The assignments took a long time but I managed with strategies that I worked out for myself. I realised that if I had time, without pressure and was able to do it at home at my on pace I could manage quite well. Sometimes in a class with distractions I found it difficult to concentrate.

I have all ways felt that I have struggled with new challenges. I couldn't just take to new routines as I felt the instructions were never clear enough. Often I felt like I was walking into new conversations at meetings and at planning sessions. I never felt part of a team. Following the thread of conversation I find difficult which leads me to feel excluded. That meant that I would often stick to the familiar routines of life as I was scared of failing. This discouraged me from trying to achieve more in life.

I'm now trying to put strategies in place to help me in both work and personal life. I would to make things clearer in my mind to improve my understanding of dyslexia and how it affects ME. I've had some support through my work and this has given me more confidence in my abilities and potential. I feel less scared of trying things because I now realise I'm not THICK, I'm probably dyslexic. I'm slowly beginning to understand more about dyslexia and the strategies and support that is out there. I now know dyslexic people can learn effectively given the right opportunities and support and there needs to be more awareness of this learning difference across society.

Adult dyslexic

---

42. A plea
"I need help"

I struggle to do maths. Reeding and right are hard. I forget words, I looz things. I need help.

11 year old boy

---

43. Adult basic education
"I have come on a lot but I still have bad days"

I thought I was always bad at English but was good at Maths. My mum tried every way for me to learn to write. But mum ended up writing all my things for me.

Once I got married William, my husband, got me to go to night classes for writing as he was doing all my writing that was where I met the teacher. She had just passed a course to tell if people were dyslexia or not.

It was with her that I found out I was dyslexic and she helped me very much. But I did not like anyone to know about it for a long time.

I got through doing some English and S.V.Q. but it took me a long time and I had a lot of support. I stopped doing things like writing and spelling and ending away back as far as I was before I got married it was very difficult for me again.

I got used to talking about being dyslexic and went back to a English class where I did some home work and have a good teacher; but I had also a lot of help from home and work the manager lets me have a late every Tuesday for my class and is very good.

I have come on a lot but I still have bad days. When I have to do courses and if I make a spelling mistake they will ask and correct it before I leave or see me later on. I enjoy doing things with my hands like knitting; crocheting, and sewing.

Adult learner

44. My arch enemy dyslexia
"like all movie villains I seem to be winning the battle"

I would like to tell you my short story about the fight I have had over the years with my arch enemy 'dyslexia'.

I started primary school in 1979 and over the years I continually got into trouble due being very frustrated at not being able to progress in my school work. As I progressed through school life I was given very little support and by primary 7 (1985) my school categorised me as a 'problem child' and sent me for a number of brain tests.

I left primary school in 1986 and started high school with my guidance teacher stating that this would be a fresh start. After the first month in high school my English teacher set a challenge to present verbally (from written homework) on what we would do if we met the giant from the 'BFG'. After presenting my homework the teacher was very impressed but asked me to stay behind after class; this was due to the fact she could not read my homework. After the class and over the next two weeks, again, I under went test and eventually it was explained I had dyslexia.

I have to say I never really understood what this was and the support I got was limited but 100% better than that of my primary school. Over the years I was ridiculed and laughed at for having a word processor (which I found hard to work) and was always asked to spell 'Cat'. I really struggled over the next four years.

I eventually left school in 1990 with very few formal qualifications and a severe lack of knowledge of the wider world. I wanted to progress in the world of sport (i.e. a PE teacher) and thought about college, however, my mother was apprehensive about this due to the last 11 years in formal education. After a lot of debate (well - my mother telling me) I undertook an apprenticeship as an electrician which was a bit more suited to me due to the lack of written English required. I worked my way through as an electrician over the next four years which was very hard and, without the support of my family and work mates, I might never have completed my course.

Well you might think that I had done well and was now a qualified electrician and still only 20 years of age but you would be wrong. I was frustrated as I found it hard to progress as most promoted jobs would required more written ability. I then found myself in a 'rut' similar to my school life and this continued until in the winter of 1995 when my father committed suicide and died. This was maybe the motivation that I needed to try and complete my goal of working in sport or at least doing something positive in my life.

In the summer of 1998 I left my job as an electrician in the shipyards and undertook a HND in Health & Fitness which enabled me to start to develop a career within sport. I soon discovered that that this was going to be a very hard career change, I was extremely out my depth and far younger students would make me feel very inadequate. It was at this time I had to really examine my own personal ambitions and decide if I really wanted to continue in this pathway. After a few days of very deep soul searching I decided that I owed it to myself to see if I could achieve my goal and be as successful as I could be. I continued my academic career by undertaking a degree in Sport Studies at University which provided a further opportunity to widen my understanding of sports/health and the industry.

In January of 2005 I was offered the job of Scottish FA Regional Manager and have to say that I shed some tears after being offered the job. After 20 years of leaving primary school with the words of teachers still haunting me that I should not aim to high because I lacked the ability to achieve these goals. I might not be rich and famous but many days I look back at my life and think, god it was hard work but am so proud of myself.

I would say to anyone that discovers they are dyslexic that its not the end of the world, yes, you will have to over come people ridiculing you but with hard work and dedication you can achieve anything you set you mind on...

Well my arch enemy is still dyslexia but like all movie villains I seem to be winning the battle...

Paul McNeill, Scottish Football Association regional manager, aged 37

---

45. Applying for jobs
"referred me back to the job centre ... over how long it took me to complete an application form."

I am Dyslexic and I have been unemployed for about 2 years. This is my 3rd and longest spell of unemployment in 10 years.

My 1st spell started with me failing my HND and ended a year later after being reassessed for Dyslexia and with me starting a degree programme. My 2nd spell started after I graduated with my degree and ended about 6 months later with me getting a temp contract in err Administration. It was a miracle that I lasted 11months.

I look for work mainly in my degree area and in other areas I would prefer it if there is a link to food and community in a job but it is not as a esstails as getting a job. I also spend some of time volunteering in various roles to get experience. I find that doing the practical stuff gives me the boost I need to attempt the things that I find challenging. So far all I have been offered is yet more voluntary work and that won't get me out of my parents' house.

My success rate:

My success rate of started to applications to completed applications is very low. Job descriptions and applications forms differ far too much and it can take ages to understand the job description and think of the right words too write.

My Success rate from completed application forms to interviews depends on what job I have applied for - if the job is clearly connected to my degree I have a very high rate of getting interviews. Outwith degree area my rate for interviews is very low and I get no interviews for the admin post the job centre encourages me to apply for.

My experience of unemployment support:

The support for the job centre and their contractors has time limit and how much support you get relays on the individual Employment Advisor and not what you need. I find I don't work well with time limits and I often go over them. In particular when faced with a 30min appointment I am frequently there for at least an hour I am unaware of how long I have been there for until I sign out or leave.

During my unemployment I have be told me my Dyslexia wasn't that bad because I had a degree. I have spent 11 months with 1 job centre contractor and 12months with another. When face with 1 on 1 appointment I went over my time slot a lot.

When I found myself in group recruitment sessions I was very easily distracted by open plan rooms and as I like to discuss the written word it gives it a greater meaning to the topic and this sometimes disturbs others because the Employment Advisor rarely had time to provide support to someone who know how to work a computer. I have been referred me back to the job centre by 1 contractor over how long it took me to complete an application form. The other cause the time limits had expired.

The job centre had an Occupational Assessment carried out on me. My Educational report was looked at there was a discussions about looking for work, the possibilities of becoming self employed the difficulties I face with becoming employed and my voluntary work. A report was written and the Job centre verdict on it was that I have lot of coping techniques. Though they have offered to refer me too anther contractor. In the mean time I keep searching and applying where I can and hoping something will come up soon.

Unemployed dyslexic, seeking work

---

46. A member of mensa
"writing was an ordeal"

School was always a contradictory place for E. Maths was a pleasure, writing was an ordeal. In the opinion of her primary school teachers, E tended to be idle and careless. In an external maths assessment taken in primary 5, she came top of the year, an achievement presented almost as an accusation. If she possessed these capabilities, why was her written work so poor? Eventually, when E was 15, a perceptive English teacher suspecting dyslexia, arranged for her to have an educational psychologist's test. This investigation resulted in extra time for exams but teachers continued to feel that E did not perform to her full potential. They really did not understand what dyslexia actually was, hardly surprising considering the meagre amount of time allocated to the subject of dyslexia in the curriculum of student teachers. The academic side of school was fairly unhappy for E and she was glad to leave. Following university, she gained a place on a graduate training programme and is currently studying to become an actuary and is a member of Mensa.

E's story told by her mother

---

47. Computer technology helps
"She left school with no formal qualifications and a lot of unhappy memories."

O can barely read and writing is confined to a few sentences which she copies out having no idea of what she is writing. She is also dyscalculic to the extent that she cannot tell the time. School was extremely difficult despite every effort made to help her. From the age of 11, her hours in school were drastically cut to 1 hour; 3 times a week and home education was undertaken. She left school with no formal qualifications and a lot of unhappy memories. Thanks to voice recognition software and a computer programme which reads scanned text, O has been able to pursue her interests. Her particular passion is politics and she is now working towards a degree with the Open University.

O's story told by her mother

---

48. Paving the way
"genetic coding and brain scanning techniques have silenced sceptics"

The year was 1923, the place, Limerick. As a special treat, a kind neighbour offered to take my father, then aged 10 for a ride in his new motor car. After the outing, the neighbour informed my grandmother, 'George could not read the road signs!' I have often wondered how she felt, for I know he used to admit that he was badly behaved at school possibly as a result of being unable to read. She loved literature and instilled in him a love of language, especially rhyme. Later he wrote poetry – proof read by my long suffering mother- as a means of passing on cherished beliefs and stories to his grandchildren.

As a small child, I remember being puzzled listening to my father read. Screwing up his eyes, he would stutter and stumble over words. Car journeys were stressful as he confused right and left and had difficulty reading signs in time to take the correct road. Yet he was an able man. A dentist by profession, he liked nothing better than to potter in the garden where he would build ornamental walls - his brick arches were the talk of the neighbourhood, to say nothing of his crazy paving. He made wonderful toys

- his piece de resistance being an incredible two storey Wendy house.

Years later, I became a primary school teacher. After my children had grown up I began to teach in a small rural primary school. Once again I was faced with a bright individual whose abilities seemed contradictory. 'Mark' was in P7. He was able to communicate fluently but when it came to putting anything down on paper it was a different matter. His writing did not flow and spelling mistakes were numerous. In due course, a psychologist was consulted and it was confirmed that his difficulties were due to dyslexia. An increasing awareness of the condition led me to look for a course of study which would increase my knowledge and make me a better teacher. It also began to dawn on me that my father had dyslexia. Alas, he died before I could discuss the matter with him.

At that time, 1991, professionals were at loggerheads about the definition of dyslexia. I needed advice so sought out Dr Catriona Collins who was well known for her work in the field at that time. She ran a part time course which led to a Royal Society of the Arts diploma for Teachers of Children with Specific Learning Difficulties. The course opened my eyes, not just to the various needs of pupils with dyslexic related difficulties. I regretted that the knowledge I gleaned during that year was not available to all teachers, for it would have transformed attitudes and teaching practices for the benefit of all, not just those with dyslexia.

I moved from the primary to secondary sector in the 1993, where I spent almost ten happy years working in a large secondary school where I was able to put into practice what I had learnt. Meanwhile researchers were discovering more about dyslexia. Developments in genetic coding and brain scanning techniques have silenced sceptics who claimed that dyslexia was 'a middle class disease' or the result of poor teaching.

I like to think my father's legacy to me has been invaluable. Unwittingly he shaped my teaching career. Rather like his crazy paving paths, the history of dyslexia has been strewn with many twists and turns and many shaky foundations. Let's hope we can step out on straight paths, built on firm foundations to a bright future where those with dyslexia reach their full potential.

A tutor

49. Dyslexia and socialising
"Dyslexia affects much more than literacy tasks"

Sometimes, I get the impression that work colleagues think I am a bit weird when it comes to socialising with them. My main difficulties with socialisation relate to memory and processing of information.

At times I have difficulty concentrating. For instance when studying, I need complete silence avoiding distractions. Therefore, in social situations, the more distractions, the harder it is to focus on conversations. An example would be a work night out to a pub. There is often:

- loud music;
- large video screens with constantly changing pictures – often different sporting events on several screens – with or without sound;
- several discussions in the work group, often with different people in the same conversation talking at once; and
- loud chatter from other people sitting close by.

Sometimes, it's difficult to concentrate after a tiring day at work, especially if I have been concentrating on processing information to solve a problem or taking part in a meeting. I then find it difficult having enough energy for a night out. The effort involved in social conversation is too much, especially if it involves teasing or leg pulling. This type of conversation involves responding quickly to witty comments. Often I miss the punch-line of a joke as I tend to take conversations literally.

Office social conversations can frequently be about current pop music or last night's TV. I have difficulty making out song lyrics on the radio, so I am unable to sing along. If the tune is particularly catchy, I can find it going round and round in my head all day, without any clue to the lyrics. I am not sure whether I have this difficulty because I have to process two bits of information – the music and the words.

Even when I can understand song lyrics, I don't always remember them. Someone once made a great statement at an adult dyslexia group meeting – my memory is like velcro that sometimes doesn't stick. For some reason some song lyrics just won't go into my long-time memory. For instance - my favourite group is U2. I watched their Glastonbury appearance this year on TV. They played my favourite song – "I Still Haven't Found What I'm Looking For". Despite the fact that I have been singing this song since it was released back in 1984 – 25 years – I still couldn't recite all the lyrics.

Generally, as I read slowly, I don't spent a lot of

time trying to read newspapers or books. I therefore tend to watch TV for facts – particularly news bulletins, documentaries, history programmes, etc. This means that instead of watching Eastenders, I'm more likely to be watching Springwatch or Coast. These latter programmes are not usually the subject of office chat!

Films are also discussed at work. I find some fast action films difficult to follow. Often I miss a bit of action which means a later part of the film doesn't make sense. Another aspect of a film which can be difficult to follow is when there is a screen of text at the start or end of a film to set at scene. I usually only manage to read half the text before it disappears off the screen, so I miss out on part of the story.

On TV, I like comic presenters like Graham Norton or Paul O'Grady as gay humour is very visual – lots of facial expressions give a clue to the fast comments and jokes. Perhaps that is why I have problems with music lyrics on the radio – there are no visuals to give me a clue as to the subject matter.

I also have difficulty remembering people's names. If I don't talk to people regularly – at least several times a week – I quickly forget names. Often I find myself running through the alphabet in my head trying to find a person's first name. I often vaguely recall if the person has a long or short name and whether it is a fairly common name. After that I just try to eliminate letters of the alphabet to recall their name. Sometimes this works, sometimes it doesn't!

Unfortunately, there is not enough awareness amongst the general public that all these difficulties are linked to dyslexia. Dyslexia affects much more than literacy tasks, but most people do not realise this.

Adult dyslexic

---

50. Find 'n out
"help'n overcoming the thinking of being thick"

I am dyslexic, I am a recovering dyslexic.

I was a late starter (later than time at school) to the dyslexia awareness revilution at the age of 36 yrs.

And the follow'n yrs have been so rich of discovery, revilations of past experinces and inexplicable psycholigical ticks and personal prefrances. Where dyslexia dealings were in play sublimary – but was thought at the time, it was part of being thick – after all, my experiances of teaching at school age confirmed this! But on the contray it was the teachers were thick - not being able to do there jobs (I transgress into moaning mood!)

Even thou dylexia has been known about for a very

long time, alas this was the 70's & 80's where I feel if they the teachers werna striking Tues-Thurs, I was striking for a wk's hols with a Mon-Fri no show. Am glad to note that this lazy bone attitude (probably a by product of my teaching experiance – my best alaby) did'nt trangres into my work ethic – my paper round was done with dedication, funding my bmxs and wkends, a nice by product.

After a chance ocarance of Dylexia indicators being observed in me & then doing Dyslexia Scotland's tick list & scoring 18 out of 20, I was chuffed – the highest ever score I had on any test.

Then with trumendous help, asistance and incuragment from Dyselia Scotland's reprisentatives, and subsiquently doing a Educational psychologist dyslexia test – highly recomended for clarity giving properties & firm base to work off. Also discovering I am 86% intelagance (the other 16% was used to get to the test!) was enpowering (hopefully not to the ego) of understanding and trusting my way of thinking, help'n overcoming the thinking of being thick – more like full of brilliant thinking that dyslexic people are gifted with. And find'n ways that aided dyslexia use.

A by product of dyslexia discovery was awareness of Mears Irlan syndrome (bit of a hypricondiral label, I feel) aka visial stress (more modern, hip and less

illness sounding). Find'n out, with me being a recipiant
of this, & doing a special eye test and by using
amber tinted lenses helped efectivaly with deal'n with
stabilizing print on page, minimizing the sore heads
- oh, the sore heads – with watchn telly, computers,
bright lights & gave extra stamina to dealing with the
stimulases of the day.

If you are dyslexic, or go onto discovering you are,
welcome to an exlusive club of Jackie Stewarts, Richard
Bransons, Winston Churchills and Kara Tointons – and
yours truely, Garry 86%.

(Had to go for a lie down after finishing this draft!!!)
Garry, adult dyslexic

---

51. Memories
"I spent years in different jobs, often being discriminated against, bullied or ridiculed".

At the age of 13 I was introverted, withdrawn, had
zero confidence and all the different forms of dyslexia
it is possible to have.

I was miserable, lonely and I wondered what on
earth was wrong with me and how my life was going to
turn out. My dad was hugely successful, our family was
well off and much was expected of me, adding even

more pressure! I was failing at school and my teachers had all but given up hope. Truth to tell, I had pretty much given up on myself. I'd been to a number of schools and at each of these I'd been bullied, ridiculed and nobody seemed to understand dyslexia. I'd even been to see a school in Llandudno, but came away realising it was not for me.

Two years in limbo followed, when I literally fell out of the system, until my dad decided to research every school in the UK to see if he could help me get the head start and motivation I desperately needed.

So, at the age of 13, I found myself leaving home and travelling some 500 miles to go to 'Brick Wall' a school in Sussex.

At such a low point in my young life, it was a daunting prospect.

Where most kids see school as something they have to do endure, I can honestly say Brick Wall was the turning point in my life!

I spent 5 years being taught in a way that I could understand.

Learning and developing, being treated with such care, kindness, trust and respect from the teachers as well as my fellow pupils, I found self-belief and intelligence that I never knew I had!

At 18, I left with the confidence and desire to

achieve and put my dyslexic symptoms to one side.

But here again, I found most employers utterly unable to understand dyslexia and the effect it had on me.

I spent years in different jobs, often being discriminated against, bullied or ridiculed. It even affected my personal life and I suffered from anxiety and panic attacks.

It was at the age of 32, after returning home from a holiday in South Africa, that I was inspired by a vision of a hippo in the water. I decided I wanted to capture the essence of the creature.

That something so clumsy and awkward on land could be so graceful and at ease in a different environment was truly inspirational to me. I suppose, in a way, it summed up how I felt as a child – awkward and out of my depth in the wrong environment for me.

I decided to design and create a series of tables, with the hippo almost submerged, just the eyes showing, peering out just above the water line. A sheet of glass defined the water surface.

The idea was an instant hit and I have never looked back.

Now, all of my work is either in the form of one-off commissions, or a series of very strictly limited works of 12, 25, 50 or 99 pieces.

Bearing in mind the help and support I was

fortunate to have and still receive, I donate the last piece on a series to charity, in the hope that I can put something back in and touch the lives of others.

Had my own life not been touched, I have no idea where I might have ended up. I never lose sight of that. I truly believe we are all born with talent and I am extremely fortunate I have been able to make the most of mine.

Today, I see my dyslexia as a gift. It helps me to see differently, think in an alternative way. Far from holding me back, it is a real asset to my creativity. I embrace differences and am passionate about diversity, equality and the natural world.

People do not always see or appreciate what they have, or what is around them until it is gone, or too late to do anything about it. Every day, as an artist and designer, taking my inspiration from the world around me, I become more and more aware of this.

I'm proud to be working close to where I grew up and still amazed by the life I am privileged to lead. I've met some of the most influential people to have lived in my generation - world leaders, rock stars, lunar astronauts, jockeys and even royalty. Not bad for a shy wee dyslexic Ayrshire lad!

My aim, through my work, is to make a contribution to those projects aimed at conservation, particularly the tiger and I am grateful to my dyslexia for taking me on a journey I neither anticipated or expected, but one that has been exhilarating and motivational.

My sincere tributes of appreciation go to those people who have helped me along the way and are still helping me to this day!

Mark Stoddart, International Designer

---

52. A long journey
"suffered a great deal of discrimination through employment"

I am now aged 46 and profoundly dyslexic. However that is not my story. I left school at age 16 with no qualifications and expectation from my family that's all I was capable of doing was working in a factory doing a basic mundane job. Even at that age I knew I was capable of doing better things but did not know what it was that held me back.

As a consequence of this when I was 18 I joined the Royal Air Force where I served for approximately 3 - 4 years. During my training it was noticed [as was the case when I was at school] this I was failing all written exams but practical exams where relatively easy. In addition to this during my training it was noticed that when under pressure I literally was 'talking to myself and when working on aircraft the airplane itself'.

As a consequence of this I was sent to a Royal Air Force Hospital for once I was told 'screening'. During my assessment at the hospital I was asked various questions for example did I hear voices, did I feel things that were not there or did I see things of which the answer was no to all of these. Latterly after these tests I did some more psycho metric tests and after evaluation I was told that originally I was being tested for suffering from schizophrenia when the case was I am profoundly dyslexic.

As a consequence of this the Royal Air Force provided relevant support and I continued with my career only leaving due to personal circumstances.

After leaving the Royal Air Force I worked in a factory for 12 years and due to the amount of bullying hid away the fact that I am dyslexic. I was always labeled by those I worked with as being 'thick, lazy, backward and slow'. The problem was when I worked in industry was that I did not have the support to encourage me to move on and do other things.

I left my job in industry - took a massive pay cut and began working in social care as a care assistant alongside studying with the Open University at the same time. During the early part of my studies I went up to Durham for a week's Summer School of which driving up there I was absolutely terrified in that I couldn't cope. Staff from the Open University provided me with a great deal of reassurance and also encouragement with regard to working what I saw students who were more capable than me. In 1996 I passed my first course with the Open University which led me to complete other courses and in due course I gave up work altogether for three years to train as a Social Worker at University.

Whilst a student at the University, academic staff questioned my ability to study even though they knew I was profoundly dyslexic. To give an example of how serious this became at one stage the Student Union became involved and legal action was threatened with regard to disability discrimination.

I eventually completed my studies with the University and qualified as a social worker- graduating and returned to my studies with the Open University of which I eventually also graduated.

As a consequence of this I am now two thirds of the way through completing my Master's degree.

Regardless of my academic qualifications my proudest moment always will be passing my first course with the Open University. This means so much to me on the basis that I had been written off by the personal family [including my father and sister] and colleagues as being incapable of achieving anything. I had suffered for many years but verbal and physical abuse when I worked in industry through bullying and also discrimination when I was a full-time student.

In addition to this I have also suffered a great deal of discrimination through employment as a social worker. From this perspective Dyslexia is a disability if a person wants to make it a disability. I know I will never find a cure for the lease by developing my own strategies with regard to dyslexia personal achievements can be completed.

Adult dyslexic, aged 46 B.A. (Hons). B.Sc (Hons – Open). Dip. App.S.S. (Open). Dip.S.W. (Salf). Dip. H.SW (Open). Cert. Man. Care. (Open). R.S.W.

53. Dyslexia is frustrating
"I try my best."

Sometimes I can't remember words. I get frustrateid. I get cross. I just strug my shoulders. At home I go out side on the trampoline because I get angry. At school I need help with language. I find it easy now. I always have to do hard work. I try my best.

11 year old boy

54. Arguing with my own brain
"tiredness never helps to keep the dyslexia monster away."

I am dyslexic; and I have been relatively successful i.e.
I achieved a BSc Honours degree. But that was over 10
years ago now and I have had a number of jobs, the
longest of which lasted for 4 years. I believe dyslexia is
an extremely complex and ever changing problem. And
it fortunately/unfortunately does not have outward
signs (or should I say reminders). Therefore authority
figures can easily forget; and perceive problems caused
by dyslexia as signs of laziness.

In clerical assistant positions I often have to work
with name and address data whilst on the phone and
using lots of office equipment. I'm sure my dyslexia really
shows up in these situations [but I can't explain it too
well] and then I tend to panic. I get so stressed about
these situations, and my apparent inability to learn
from my mistakes and avoid the same mistakes over and
over again. I then have trouble sleeping at night. Which
means I'm tired from the start of the day and tiredness
never helps to keep the dyslexia monster away.

When I was little, I was unable to learn to read and
when I tried to write I was so upset/frustrated by the
school environment that my sweaty hands smudged

what I had written so much that no-one could read what I had written. My mother could see there was a problem. She says she could see my intelligence in everything else I did and could not understand why school was such a problem for me. But the teachers just would not listen to my parents. My parents got me diagnosed at their own expense. And it was only then that they were taken seriously. Then I did manage to learn to read through specialised teaching. But the frustration has never gone away. That's frustration I have with my own brain to make it learn and to believe it can learn. Hands up who has ever managed to win an argument with they're own brain whilst trying to solve a complex coded message?

My discomfort at primary school was made worse by the fact that it was the school bus driver who gave me one of my first cruel names in the form of 'Dozy'. Of course anyone who is trying incredibly hard to learn something that everyone else can do relatively easily; whilst being called 'dozy' will be profoundly affected.

Why is it that it is the pupils who are struggling; who get the worst teachers? When I was in 3rd year maths (foundy/general); we hadn't had a steady teacher all year. This awful ineffective teacher who let the class run riot for weeks; came in and laid down the law. Fair enough! If the teacher had actually come when I put up my hand right at the beginning of the lesson it would have been OK. But it all ended badly with me getting a punishment exercise just for asking for help. And the rubbish teacher allowing the rest of my class to hack away at my dignity by shouting at me to cry. Anyway after this year of utterly ineffective teaching we were given a national exam. I remember being disappointed in my 48% score. But after that the head of the maths department came running up to me saying I'd done really well. I remember saying "But I failed!" She said "But what did the rest of your class get?" It turned out everyone else got less than 20% for the most part.

So I guess by that point I'd got pretty good at teaching myself!

When I was doing my RPR in higher English my teacher accused me of plagiarism and of downloading it from the internet. And when I insisted that I hadn't she made me do it again as she said if she submitted it the exam board would say I'd cheated as my examination work would be rubbish in comparison.

I hate signing-on and being treated like someone who has no drive and/or ability; and when I'm lucky they send me to agencies set up for the physically disabled. These agencies rarely have a clue about dyslexia and other unseen disabilities and yet those are the people who are referred to them for the most part.

Adult dyslexic, female

55. Struggle from school to university
"achieved through personal hard work, parents who battled and supported me and with the assistance of a tutor"

I am the second child with an 8 and a half year age gap between myself and my older brother. Both my parents were the first generation in their families to attend university and both ended up with very high jobs. Even though they were very high fliers, me and my brother were always a priority as well as taking us to ballet, scouts music lessons etc. My parents had to fight to ensure my brother's health and education were catered for as he was born with a physical difficulty which is on going and he has been a wheelchair user since early High School.

I went to Primary school when I was 4 because my birthday coincided with the cut off. So I was one of the youngest in the class. In P1 and P2 I was quickly placed into a very low reading group and the other groups spent lots of time with the teacher reading and I felt like the time spent was cut short because of the group struggling. I loved books at this stage and it was hard to be left behind. By the time I was in P4 I remember how much I struggled through my lessons. The teachers thought it was just because I was meant to be the year below. But it wasn't till P4 when I was diagnosed with being dyslexic. Because I was struggling my parents sought out an independent dyslexic tutor who developed my skills through to High school.

High school was easier in some ways because I could find my own feet but it was a struggle with the teachers because I was the first dyslexic pupil to come through with such developed coping mechanisms. I was placed in lower classes and generally had to fight to get the grades I deserved. In English I was in the lowest set but I did get to sit the credit standard grade and I got a high 2! My dad had sought out special exercise classes and this helped a little with general balance and coordination which friends and family said they could see improvements.

Harry Potter! This was the first book I read on my own and I think it was these which got me back into using my imagination which were both skills which I felt had been crushed at Primary School. JK Rowling continues to inspire me through not only her books but also through Pottermore.

Since then I have been to university and have graduated with a 2:1. This has been achieved through personal hard work, parents who battled and supported

me and with the assistance of a tutor from age 7
through to age 18 with a short break of a term when I
settled into High school.

Young adult dyslexic

---

56. A tutor's support
"the combination of high ability (IQ 150) and the severity of her dyslexia proved challenging"

I have known X since 1997 when I began teaching
her as part of my training for the R.S.A. Diploma for
Teachers of Learners with Specific learning Difficulties
(Dyslexia). At the time I was teaching in two High
Schools, as a teacher of Learning Support at one school
and with responsibility for a Dyslexia Initiative at the
other. The combination of roles led me to a deeper
understanding of Dyslexia and a greater appreciation of
the needs of the individual. It also highlighted for me
the difficulties experienced by dyslexic pupils within
secondary education.

My priorities in working with X were to raise
and maintain her self-esteem as well as to provide
strategies for improving reading, writing and spelling.
Interventions for reading have included the Toe-by-Toe

programme and Stride Ahead, after having tried other methods. Subject support has also been important, as have brain training, self-development and memory training (visualisation). For a long time, support and teaching for maths and science were provided by family.

Support was a particular feature in the High School that she attended, however the combination of high ability (IQ 150) and the severity of her dyslexia proved challenging and she was often placed in bottom sets.

The following specialised support interventions have been undertaken in addition to ten years of weekly dyslexia tutoring for varying periods of time beginning with 45 minutes in the early years and eventually increasing to 90 minutes.

- Johanssen Sound Therapy
- NHS Speech and Language Therapist
- Occupational Therapy (including keyboarding skills)
- Computer and specialised software then laptop
- Keyboarding course (specialised company) small group teaching for a week
- Optician-coloured overlay
- DDAT (now closed)
- Special Exam Arrangements (reader, scribe, transcription with correction, use of computer

The interventions which provided the greatest

improvement were Toe-by-Toe and colour coding speech therapy as well as training in computer use and software predictive text. Microsoft Word linked to the Kurzweil speech synthesiser software made an additional contribution. Parental and extended family support, high intelligence and developing self-esteem have all played a major role in her success and recent graduation with an upper second class degree.

A tutor

---

57. Keeping a sense of humour
"drill a hole for the skin"

A couple of humorous dyslexia stories re my hubby who is dyslexic.

When I was away at Uni my husband (then boyfriend) would write me letters (this is before the days of email and text!). His first letter to me started "Dear Sweatheart". I realised he had meant to call me his Sweetheart, but to this day I am still his Sweatheart!

Recently we were getting our bathroom done up. My husband left me a note "Ask the plumber to drill a hole for the skin". All morning I was wondering where in the bathroom was the 'skin' and why it needed a

hole. Only when the plumber arrived did I realised my
husband had meant the sink!
Wife of husband with dyslexia

---

58. Embarrassed by dyslexia
"even keeping this quietly from my wife and kids"

I always knew I had problem with dyslexia especially
reading and spelling. I thought that I was stupid.
When in my teens I was struggling at school I did
not have good grades so I didn't get into uni so
try collage but dropout after 2 months. I was an
embarrassment to my family because all the kids in
the Chinese community about my age was going in uni
or collage. After all this I started woking with my dad
in the Chinese takeaway in my comfort zone. Even
keeping this quietly from my wife and kids, I started
looking up on the internet for information on dyslexia.
It was hard to find the confidence to go support group.

Support Group: At first I did not no what to
expect from the support group. I thought group
would improve my reading and spelling. But is
confidence building mainly I think. Is good to know
that other people same problem as me. The group

has been good for me give strategies to coping with dyslexia. It's been good with group especially when you have a good leader that give a lot information. I try to go to all the meeting.

The big plus: Is for improving my reading and spelling. I do this every wednesday morning for 2 hours. It's a wee bit like going back to school. With out the hard teachers.

I hope you can understand what i have written and it only taking me 2.30 hours to write this. LOL
Adult dyslexic, male

---

59. Identified with dyslexia too late
"found out I was dyslexia 5 year a go sins then Iv found out my mum was, so was her sister"

Hi my story born 1947, was adopted in 1951. Schooling was hard did not pass 11 pluss, sent to a school 15 miles from where I lived. Became a good runner to stop being picked on. From school to work at 16 in local government doing stabs, tar mac, street cleaning to driving. Doing papper work was hard but got some help, copy street name was a other way I did it. Wife had heart attack 2 stroke under 40, we got a teen age girl to bring up with all that takes. Lucky I ad family with girl in to help how girl was 13 at me time she id her mum I was on my to the R.T.A. but did not now it was my wife. Tock a job in town so I get home at meal time and school times. I tock early retmet at 55. 2 year later we move to Scotland so my girl go to collage in Angus 2002. Sad she is singal mum to 2 children one 7 other 5 started P1 this year. Iv do some work up here school patrol and kictchen porter. Now full time carer. I found out I was dyslexia 5 year a go sins then Iv found out my mum was, so was her sister thay where sent to a hospital in Bristol . Now I'm looking to start a local brach for Dyslexia Scotland in September and next year I'm 65. 2 year later going to New Zealand see wife brother.

Adult dyslexic

---

60. Quotes from pupils with dyslexia

"The you nit helps you with dislexya."

"I get help with my byslexia."

"I feld nervous before I started the unit. I have improved writing and spelling the unit is lots of fun. If you come to the unit don't worry because it is lots of fun and it will help you."

"My writing is definitely better! My spelling is much better! When I saw the difference – wow!"

"I sometimes still don't pay attention but I do most of the time. I do get fidgety. I think I can sort things out more in my head so amn't so muddled up."

"The ruler stops the letters moving. They can get a bit fuzzy. I use it here but I don't use it at school because I think it makes me look stupid."

"I can write my retell all by myself now!"

"I'm dyslexic but I just come in and out of it!"

"Just go to Mrs --------- and she'll sort you out!" (said to a Headteacher!)

Pupils from the Specific Learning Difficulties Support Service

61. Specific learning difficulties support service
"how lucky we are to have such provision in our area",

Extract from letter to Cluster Headteachers about SpLDSS (Specific Learning Difficulties Support Service)

"Having just completed my first year at the SpLDSS Unit I feel compelled to feed back on our experiences and to continue to champion its cause ....

I simply want to emphasise how lucky we are to have such provision in our area, and highlight that its retention is mainly due to psychology involvement coupled with a proper constitution. In my opinion the SpLDSS fulfils the inclusion agenda: despite pupils being partly educated out with their regular school environment, the intensive literacy teaching and support ensures pupils are more included in the long term. Not only can they access the curriculum more easily, they feel better about their learning difference and can recognise the strengths they have as a result. The structure of multi-sensory activities, step-by-step teaching and over-learning, all within a nurturing setting, combine to build pupils' skills to a more competent level. Above all, how pupils view themselves

and compare themselves to others, alters: shaky self-esteem becomes a little less so; hidden excuses and avoidance tactics slowly adapt to the use of effective strategies to positively circumnavigate trickier areas; confidence increases. Gradually and cumulatively the pupils learn to support one another and become a cohesive, co-operative group. .... I feel proud and privileged to be allowed to teach such extraordinary children."
Teacher

---

62. Wishing to be like everyone else
"what he can achieve when he makes use of the support"

I had worked for a few years with a young lad, who has dyslexia, and was then in P7. He had worked really hard and had become a reasonably good reader. I had told his class teacher that I thought he could pass a level D reading test before going to High School. There were 'alternative assessment arrangements' in place for this lad, where he could read the paper aloud; have extra time and have the questions read to him and scribed if necessary. When I was next in school the teacher told me quietly that he had failed the first paper quite dramatically.

I asked if the arrangements had been put in place and she said no because he had wanted to do the test 'like everyone else!'. Whilst I appreciated where he was coming from, he had no difficulty understanding text, only de-coding it and focussing long enough to read it properly. The arrangements are designed to ensure he has the opportunity to reach his full potential but the side effect of that is that he feels 'different' from his peers.

I had a chat with him and convinced him that if he sat the test 'like everyone else' he might fail but if he uses the arrangements entitled to him he would pass 'like everyone else!'

He had already started to read the paper by himself but he reluctantly agreed to read it aloud to me.

The first line read; 'Some people consider mosquitoes to be pests.' He read mosquitoes fine but read 'pests' as 'pets'. He then re-read this line and said; 'Oh, I wondered who would have mosquitoes as pets?'

It's the small words that get you every time but they can change the meaning of the whole text!

This lad went on to pass his level D reading with almost full marks, making full use of the alternative arrangements available and entitled to him.

I only hope this made him realise how clever he is

and the importance of the arrangements and what he can achieve when he makes use of the support he is entitled to.

A support for learning teacher

---

63. Dyslexia and me
"dyslexia isn't confined to the written word"

I have spent most of my life not knowing that I am dyslexic. When I found out at age 41 I initially thought that my dyslexia could not have been spotted earlier because there was no evidence of it in my family.

There had been no obvious literacy difficulties for me at school and when I discovered my dyslexia I was working as a lecturer with two degrees and was about to complete a post graduate qualification. I had also been one half of a comedy scriptwriting partnership with some success at the BBC. I wondered how typical my experience was.

It was only when I studied the research on dyslexia and the high achievements of other dyslexics that I began to understand that dyslexia isn't confined to the written word, but can shape the way a person takes in, processes and gives out any type of information. I began to see that there had been evidence of dyslexia in my family - I just hadn't recognised the signs.

I grew up in north Wales, after my whole family moved there from Manchester. So we put my grandmother Olive's hilarious and varied mispronunciations of Welsh place names down to her being English, as well as her age. I now remember that she also mispronounced many other everyday words. Her favourite tipple was Chincano By Janco, we ate cumcubers in our salad and we enjoyed a trip to the cimena. We normalised her 'Olivisms' into regular 'family speak' and were accepting when she laughed but clearly hadn't got the joke. I now realise that she was probably displaying the phonological and auditory processing difficulties associated with dyslexia.

My grandmother had limited literacy, rarely taking on more than a Mills and Boon novel. In the past I put her less sophisticated reading choice down to her schooling. Now I see her reading limitations in the context of how dyslexicly brilliant she was as well: she could knit an Arran cardigan at break-neck speed whilst criticising the plot line of Coronation Street, without dropping a stitch or looking down. She once told me (as I watched with awe the blur of the needles and her steady gaze at the television) that she didn't need to follow the pattern, as she could see the cardigan in her head. She was a visual thinker

– another clue to her dyslexia.

By looking from a new perspective I have learned to spot the strengths and weaknesses that I share with my grandmother. This in turn has helped me to recognise the pattern of dyslexia in my own children; there is no chance that they will grow up not being aware of their dyslexia.

I am still wondering how typical my story is. This is because many of my generation of school leavers were missed and therefore still don't know they are dyslexic. Their stories have yet to be heard. We need greater knowledge and wider understanding of the variety of ways that dyslexia shapes our daily interactions, so this group of people can begin to recognise it in their own lives.

Jan Halfpenny, dyslexia consultant for business and education

---

64. Being dyslexic
"We are speshal in ore own way"

Being dyslexic it is harder to read, spell and copy. telling the time is hard to
I get mixed up With the numbers.
I feelt like I couled not keep up with my class and I

was sad but now I am at the speshel class I am happy:)

My friend ben has a brother couled Sam and he is dyslexic and he is leving school to be an enganer. I wouled like to be an enganer becus I like cars and i am good With engens.

At home I get help from my family by reading to them if you read evry day you be cume good at it and if you right evry day you will good at it to.

11 year old boy

---

65. A reflective story
"I myself, was as naïve about dyslexia, as they were."

The term dyslexia is derived from the Greek (dys), meaning impaired, and (lexis), meaning word, but to be brutally honest, the terms fails to express the true nature of the syndrome that it embodies, only scratching the surface of what dyslexia fundamentally is. Sadly, not only the name has fallen under scrutiny over the years. For some even today, still question dyslexia's very existence.

I, myself, have struggled, with the affects of dyslexia, and on first hearing that it had been questions, it had puzzled me, for I found it quite naïve, that someone could deny something I clearly had, but as time went on I began to realise that, I myself, was as naïve about dyslexia, as they were. Even though I knew the basics and even though I had it, I still didn't really, know, or fully understand it.

It wasn't until my late teens, early 20s when the un-believable happened, for the first time in my life I began, to not only write but enjoy it; now, back at school I hated writing, I avoided it like the plague but for some reason now I can't seem to live without it. It was only around this time that I began to study and read up on dyslexia, and the more I discovered and learnt of dyslexia and its complexities, not only did begin to get a better to understanding of myself but I also came to realises why after one hundred years some still question it for the right reasons or not.

I would argue, as would many, that the most problematic period for dyslexics is schooling. I have read many experiences of dyslexic pupils, and all seem to arrive at the same conclusion. Both secondary and primary schools lack the support to deal with children or young adults with dyslexia, and through the lack of support we tend to see the majority of dyslexic pupils following either of two paths, that of common passive classroom behaviour or aggressive classroom behaviour, which is not acceptable in academia and inevitability leads to such consequence as expulsion and exclusions.

I, myself, in fact tended to wonder back and forth down the two paths when faced with the horrible task of reading allowed in English for instance; if sitting in near silence didn't keep under the teacher's radar, and the excuse of not bringing ones glasses to school didn't capitalize, then I resorted to doing whatever I could possibly do to prevent being forced into reading in front of my peers, even if that meant getting thrown out of class or indeed the Fear, fear of being laughed at, fear of being excluded, there was not contest at the time I left school at fifteen no standard grades or equivalents.

But when speaking about school and that period of my life I cannot do it without mentioning my mother. I cannot begin to express, how profoundly grateful I am of the support, my mother has gave throughout my life. For if it were not for the efforts that my mother went to, the hours of struggle, and sometimes even tears, I could not be the man I am today, I could never have enjoyed the beauty for life for all it is, I would have stood as an uneducated un-examined life among many.

Night after night at home, sitting me down, to do, toe by toe, relentlessly, trying and trying after each time I through back in her face. Her efforts were out of this world and all so that I could get an equal chance in life.

James Frederick Kerr, young adult

66. Goals in sight
"not every boss/ employer would be so understanding"

It wasn't until I was going into second year at University that I was tested for dyslexia, and that was how I found out about it. After reading a note in my doctors surgery, I thought that what they had described sounded like me, and from there I contacted University. I was 27 at the time, and felt relief because I had always felt inadequate, and stupid. I never really did well at school, and my family had brought me up as "the stupid one." They still treat me this way and deny that I even have it.

I ended up dropping out of my first degree because I got really stressed and anxious. The self doubt of my up bring had left me quite scard. Both stress, anxiety and self doubt are apparently prevalent in people with dyslexia making University very daunting. After another couple of unsuccessful attempts at studying, I finally managed to achieve an HND in Accounting and now I have 2 exams to sit until I pass my degree.

Last year, at 37, I was diagnosed with ADHD. Apparently a third of people with the disorder have a second underlying condition such as dyslexia, an anxiety disorder or other intertwined conditions.

I was given a grant whilst at college to fund a computer, and I always get extra time in exams, but I have never received any other help with either of my conditions. I am so close to achieving some of my goals, but I have often felt quite frustrated at my lack of progression in my career, and life.

In my present work place, I have been open and honest about my disabilities, with my boss, and a couple of my colleagues. I felt like I had taken a risk though, because not every boss/ employer would be so understanding. Again, in a work situation, these disorder manifest in stress, and last winter I ended up being of sick for 4 weeks because of this. This was not the first time that I had suffered like this, as this has happened several times in the past and I have end up losing jobs or dropping out of a course.

Being dyslexic makes most things in life harder but not impossible, and along with the negatives come some positives. For example I am very creative, I draw and I'm writing a book. It may not be grammatically perfect but the creative idea is on paper. I am also highly, verbally articulate, I am determined, and have had to be in order to achieve.

Dyslexia and ADHD have held me back in the past but now that I am older, and understand myself better, I am not allowing myself to be held back anymore. I am aware of my limitation so I am taking small steps at a time, and achieving. Now that I am starting to experience success, it is only making me more determined, and I just want to push myself as far as I can go.

People, in the work place and the general population need to be made more aware of dyslexia and what it means. Most people still think it's about bad spelling and reading, but they have no idea of the other difficulties like poor short term memory, and lack of organisational skills etc. I am very forgetful and scatter brain which can make for a difficult day, some colleagues can be cruel at times, and on bad days, I can take it very personally. These days though I am better at ignoring it and letting it wash right over. If the average Joe had half of what I have had to deal with, I don't think most would cope, so on better days I can almost allow myself to be proud of my achievements.

Adult dyslexic, female

67. Facing up to your dyslexia
"I nearly didn't get into Australia when I first played for Scotland as I had copied another player's entry form including his name and address"

School days we are told by our parents, should be the happiest days of our lives, but for me they were dark and miserable. Having difficulty with reading and writing caused me to fall behind in other subjects. I was the butt of other children's jokes and was anxious most of the time. I felt sick every time I walked into school, but I never played truant. However some of the time I was genuinely ill through the stress of just going to school. For most Dyslexics, school life can be difficult, but my school life was over 30 years ago and things have changed a lot since then and for the better as teachers are now more aware of Dyslexia and help is at hand.

I never spoke about my illiteracy problems to anyone. I harboured it within myself. My release was on the rugby pitch; playing rugby was something I was good at.

Back then, diagnosis was difficult to obtain as awareness of Dyslexia was not widely known about. It was not until I was sixteen that a history teacher who was involved in remedial classes at her house diagnosed me with Dyslexia. It was relief to find out what the problems with illiteracy had been.

However diagnosis, didn't mean cure and there was only so much that this kind teacher could do. I realised that the struggle would continue.

Throughout my life I became very good at concealing my Dyslexia but you can only do this for a certain amount of time. As you become an adult you take on more responsibilities. Reading and completing forms is part of everyday life but they were often major hurdles for me. I nearly didn't get into Australia when I first played for Scotland as I had copied another player's entry form including his name and address. The immigration officer thought I had got the wrong form and gave me a new one, and helped me fill it in; maybe he could see that I was struggling. There are some kind people.

My wife Gabby has been hugely supportive of my Dyslexia. She forced me to face up to it and gave me the confidence to do so. I enrolled in a programme to help me tackle my Dyslexia. At first it was detrimental to my rugby but then it enhanced my skills. At the age of 30 I finally learnt my vowels. I now enjoy reading the paper over a cup of tea, and can fill out forms on my own; something I never thought I would do.

One thing I learned is not to hide the fact that you have Dyslexia. These days there is a lot of help at hand and with hard work you can overcome it. Do not shy away from reading books. I am passionate about the value of literacy to enable you to have a normal life.

There are many well-known dyslexics from Hollywood actors, to pop stars, athletes, entrepreneurs, poets and chefs! This shows that with the right help, dyslexics can achieve great things.

Kenny Logan, international rugby player, 70 caps for Scotland

---

68. The worst days of my life
"The pain and humiliation of school were about to implode"

My earliest memories involve a teacher who hated left handed children. She took to hammering my offending hand with a wooden pencil box. Learning numbers and words filled me with fear and horror to the point I developed a bedwetting problem and my hair fell out. My dad taught me to read, without him I would have been illiterate.

My writing and counting were very poor and soon I entered the remedial stream we moved around a lot with my dad's job. Each new school promised new hope only for this to be dashed by a run of teachers who claimed I was useless and non academic. My mum and dad said I was bright, I was a good orator. But this fell on deaf ears. Year in year out was the same humilation and rejection. I felt useless, my confidence was on the floor. I was bullied a lot by teachers and peers and then I reached my teens.

The pain and humiliation of school were about to implode even now I walk by my old high school I see it as a house of pain and correction. Not a place of learning and advancement as it should be. My English teacher spotted dyslexia in me, I was assessed at 14, my school didn't recognise Dyslexia. My parents fought a battle but were told I was non academic and lazy. They must have felt gutted to get the assessment but to be told that dyslexia was a middle class construct invented by parents who could not accept there children were not academic.

My confidence collapsed and I had a nervous breakdown at 15 I was hospitilised in 1982. My memories of this period in my life still haunt me. I left school at 16. Many people will think I'm painting a negative picture of school, the truth is school was a dark place for me to be. I left school in '82 when unemployment was rife. I ended up in the cycle of unemployment then onto job creation schemes my dyslexia stalking me like an old dog. I didn't want to accept Dyslexia, I felt useless, stupid, I was a no hoper.

At 22 I entered College after my Job Creation supervisor saw that I loved helping people. I gained three O levels and an SVQ in social care, I also won a cross college award it was incredible achieving for the first time in my life. I'll never forget the buzz of success I drank it like a thirsty man in the desert. I now dreamt of University this was to take me ten years to achieve.

I applied to college, I completed a one year Diploma in Scottish Studies this was a pivotal year in my life. I got into University, I could not believe it I cried like a baby when I got the letter of acceptance, I thought they had given the wrong guy ie me a place. Four years later in summer of 05 I stepped up to collect an MA Hons in Scottish Ethnology. It was proud and emotional day in the University hall, but tinged with sadness as dad wasn't there, he had died and he taught me to read when the school had dumped me in the remedial stream.

I returned a year later to collect a post Grad in community Education. My post grad year was hell on earth it was like being back at school in terms of my treatment as a dyslexic. We have so much to do to stop Dyslexics being treated as brutally as I was that year. I believe the darkness that enveloped me at teacher training college must have torn holes in my marriage and family life. Dyslexia can cause devastation if left unassessed.

The last four years have seen me working as a tour guide. Sadly I lost my job due to ill health I was diagnosed with Chronic fatigue syndrome. I had been developing as a Storyteller in my spare time, I am now accredited and hope to develop this on a freelance basis. I also volunteer, I am kept busy, I don't give up easily. I will never forget the pain of my schooling. It's crucial children get assessed early so as to avoid the devastation adult dyslexics of my generation faced. I have found my voice, it's taken my entire life to reach this point. It's ironic I am now a Storyteller. I was blessed with a good command of the English language and a great long term memory. Life can be incredibly sad but it can also be beautiful. Dyslexia has forged me in a funny kind of way I am proud of this.

Colin Williamson, aged 45

69. Muddle or Muggle?

I love to sing, know all the tunes,

Love to dance and do gymnastics, that's magic,

I've got rhythm and can rhyme,

But don't ask me to read, I prefer to mime.

It takes me time, please can you see,

Reading is tiring, makes my head hurt

To 'see' the words and hear in my head

And match them up to be read.

Why is it I can do some things on cue,

But still confuse 'b' and 'd', 'p' with 'q'?

I can be at sixes and sevens with my 6's and 9's

3's and 5's and 2 can be too.

Then there's, there, they're and their

And to, two and too.

Why is everything such a struggle?

Could I be a Dyslexic Muggle?

A tutor

---

70. No confidence
"big thanks to my old guidance teacher"

I'm a 25 year old person, who is dyslexic and I'm struggling to have confidence in myself.

When I was a kid, I was brought up badly with my parents fighting, that's mostly due to my dad having a lot of drink in him and always fighting my mum. Sometimes, I had to phone the police a few times to try and break them up. But also my dad beat me up when I was younger and thanks to him, he knocked all the confidence out of me.

I was also bullied in school because of my disabilities, because I had a speech therapist because I couldn't say some words properly. It was at High School, I finally got some help, with big thanks to my old guidance teacher, in which he started me back on the road to success.

I was getting a reader and a scribe for when I had exams and felt better because I had got some 1's and 2's in music and maths.

I've been looking for a job now for the last 9 or so months and I'm in no luck at all. Also heard that being dyslexic, its more harder getting a job when you're dyslexic and I also have flat feet so I can't stand up for long otherwise my feet hurts.

I also do voluntary work, working for disabled kids and adults every Thursday night. What we do is play sports with them like football, hockey, basketball etc and then going in the swimming pool to learn the kids or adults how to swim. I've been doing that now for over 8 years and I've really enjoy it and have no plans of quitting!

I'm also avid on playing sports, I play darts semi-professionally but really having no confidence in myself because of my dad, I just feel every time I play darts, I always expect to lose when I should be confident and thinking I should be winning.

I do love motor sports, I first started watching Formula 1 about 15 years ago and watching the old Formula 1 days of Jackie Stewart, Niki Lauda, Aryton Senna etc, I also love watching BTCC, Nascar etc... even motor bike racing too! That's something I enjoy and take my mind away from what's happened to me ever since I was a kid.

I'm doing something about my confidence and other stuff that's to do with dyslexia. It's something that's not healed within a few days, it takes months or even years to get my confidence back and helping out with dyslexia too.

Adult dyslexic

71. A junior international ice hockey star

"If they are doing a new drill, Josh makes sure he is positioned half way down the line so he can see the drill in action"

Josh, who is now 15 years old, was identified quite early in P3 with dyslexia. He had already been diagnosed with Tourettes and sight difficulties at the age of 5. Josh remembers at this age knowing that he was not keeping up with the other kids in the class and feeling relieved to find out that it was Dyslexia that was causing his problems both in literacy and maths. Josh was supported through-out primary school with extra tuition and he did master the art of reading.

Josh has been a passionate Ice Hockey player since the age of 5! His early training and games were played at Kirkcaldy and Dundee ice rinks. Pretty soon people noticed that Josh was not just becoming a talented hockey player but he also had a determination to continually improve his skills.

By the age of 11 Josh had progressed to High School. He was now an accomplished reader and was getting by using phonetic spelling. His dyslexia was now causing him the most problems in Maths, where he struggled to learn new formulas on top of shaky number foundations. He was also finding foreign languages difficult due to not fully understanding the rules of English, never mind French! Josh was also realising he had some organisational difficulties now that he had all these books and classes to attend. However his Ice Hockey playing was going from strength to strength! Josh had 'out-grown' what Scotland had to offer in way of training and the difficult decision was made to look abroad for further training.

Austria was opening a new Hockey School in 2009. Josh and his family flew to Austria so he could take part in the trials. Out of 50 hopefuls, Josh showed enough talent and the right attitude to become one of the 18 (only 3 from UK) founder students.

The students here work towards earning the International Baccalaureate at the end of 4 years. Josh continued to work hard in his academic subjects but was offered little in the way of support for his dyslexia. He did find the strict regime and living independently helped to improve his organisational skills. He also became fluent in German thanks to his room mate, who is now fluent in English thanks to Josh!

By the end of his second season in Austria, Josh had met the president of Austria and played in Italy, Switzerland, Germany, Slovakia and Slovenia. Despite an obvious talent in ice hockey, his dyslexia still creates a challenge for Josh. If the coach writes up a 'play' on the board in the changing room it takes Josh longer than most to take it in; he has to run it through in his mind but won't fully understand it until he had acted it out on the ice. Also if they are doing a new drill, Josh makes sure he is positioned half way down the line so he can see the drill in action rather than having to do it first with only the oral instructions to work from. So, having spent the last two years perfecting his sport, what is next for Josh?

Josh has just started school at the Ontario Hockey Academy in September 2011 under part-scholarship scheme. This school values academic achievement as highly as athletic excellence and Josh will continue with his general studies. This school does recognise Josh's learning difficulties and have already promised to support his learning.

He has a clear plan of being offered a college or university scholarship through his Ice Hockey; earning himself a degree and taking up a position as a coach or a sports psychologist. Unless he is spotted in Canada by a scout and given the chance to live his dream and play in the NHL. Watch this space!!

Josh's story told by his parents

72. Living and working with dyslexia
"it affected was my ability to do my job"

I've always had problems with writing and spelling and that often made life difficult and caused me to be made fun of. As I got older the problem seemed to get bigger because, as an adult, I had to contend with a lot more writing. My work in the community meant that I had to attend meetings, take notes and write reports. When it came to writing letters I was stuffed – I just didn't know how or where to start and I knew that I would have the comments of others to deal with once they'd seen my efforts. They made me feel that I wanted to just crawl under the table.

Another thing it affected was my ability to do my job as a sign writer.

I managed to do the course at college but when it came to painting signs for customers, I'd often have painted the wrong words or spellings so I wasted a lot of time and money. When I worked as a painter and decorator the dyslexia made it difficult to work out how much materials I would need and how to cost the job. I also worked as a bus driver and had to deal with the struggle of filling in traffic reports and taking down phone messages – that's always difficult.

When it came to the time when my kids would ask

for help with their homework, I'd often hear myself saying, "go and ask your mother". I did try to help if I could but I also often tried to avoid it without it looking as if I was pushing them away.

I've recently done a lot of work at an adult education class to improve my reading writing and spelling. I've even got a few certificates and am beginning to be able to plan my writing and put things together in such a way that it makes sense. This has given me the confidence to be able to send letters and take notes if and when I need to.

Adult learner

---

73. Learning support and scribes
"learning to find coping tools"

I was very lucky to be found to be dyslexic at a very early age. I suppose almost by definition writing and reading are never going to be the preferred communication forms for dyslexics, so in order to make this easier to write for me and easier I hope to read, or readable, I will keep it short and in the form of staged memories about my personal account.

The first memory is not my own, it is that of my mother who was greeted by a teacher of mine, when

I had just started school at about 5 years. Having "mastered" copying the letters in English, I had decided to "move on" so when asked what the random lines I had made where, I reported that it was Chinese.

The next is my own I was lucky to be given Learning Support from the age of about 7. At the time I knew it was very useful and since leaving school I know it was crucial, but Learning Support had to be fitted in to the school programme, so I went off to be "supported" when other people were doing things like PE or Personal Social Development. I did go to some of these "wonder" activities and so know full well what I was missing, but even running in the rain was more fun that sitting in a room one on one trying to learn to sound words out.

I was wisely suggested against doing higher English or History. I did and don't care about not doing Higher English; I know a lot of people who sweated blood to scrap a pass. So I did a Higher in Classical Studies and I think that 80% did it as they also were "not right for Higher English", and we had a great time. The memory that I wanted to share was that each week the teacher would read out the essay title for that week and each week I handed in an essay. It was not until about 2/3s into the year that the teacher asked me why my title was always different from the one he read out. I said that it was due to the fact that sometimes I could not spell the exact word(s) used, so I used different words that meant the same thing. He explained that he chose his words very carefully and so would print off the titles for the whole class. The first week he did this we were grateful as everyone preferred not to have to write down the long titles with long words in it.

For all or most of the exams I have ever taken I have had them scribed for me. This is a skill I have learnt and has been very useful to me in a number of ways. Due to the nature of university exams as I was "disabled" I was not allowed to have an exam not on the ground floor, and had extra time and a reader and a script. So once memorable time I met my Scribe and we walked to the "eaxm room" so I said that is ionic, and she asked what was. She then refused to let me read the questions myself as she was my reader and opened all the windows as it was so hot, this meant that when everyone else came out of the exam and passed the room I had about 15mins of chatter for my 30mins extra time. After the exam I asked if I could have the "eaxm room" sign and she asked the invigilator who said that of course I could have a misspelled sign, and that he was sorry that it had been put up in the first place. I don't think she ever saw the irony or funny side.

So my personal account of dyslexia can be summed up as. Learning to find coping tools (I would say a word meaning a system of parts to perform a function but I can't spell it) and also try and see the funny side. It's an old joke but dyslexia rules KO; I think it makes me a natural listener and a creative mind.

Dyslexic male, aged 28

---

74. A special family
"Lith is hard for me

I am speshl in my way.

I have dift difculs spelling, reding and clocks

At home my mum, my uncle and my borther are dyslexic to

My mum and my DaD helps me with homework and stursh.

I forget stush and lot and i lost things.

I get triylerd wen I do long jodes

I teay hard alot

Lith is hard for me. Over pepll golit to the name is Tiger Woods and Will Smist. the are famus

10 year old girl

---

75. A success story
"if a different route has to be taken it does not mean that goals cannot be achieved"

Our daughter Johanne seemed settled in Primary School. However, our awareness of dyslexia was raised through difficulties her brother experienced and it became apparent that she too might be dyslexic. At age 7 she was assessed at the Dyslexia Institute and dyslexia was confirmed. We agonised over the decision whether to send her for 2 hours tuition a week at the Dyslexia Institute. Her teacher was horrified at the suggestion and I felt that it would be emotionally too costly for Johanne to remove her from school against her teacher's wishes.

Johanne's dyslexic difficulties escalated during her adolescent years and she left school as soon as she turned 16. Her ambition had always been to work with children and Child Care seemed an obvious career choice. Her National Certificate year in college was very challenging. The lecturers just would not look beyond the poor writing, spelling, grammar etc. One lecturer even ripped up her work and put in the bin. She was not going to be awarded a pass but she had completed all the assignments so she was reluctantly accredited with a NC Childcare. However, the College would not let her follow the Higher National course saying she would not cope with the written work. I can still visualise her lying on our couch just distraught!

Picking herself up Johanne started job hunting and was accepted as a nursery assistant in a Private Nursery. She gained Child Care qualifications through a private training Company in Glasgow. Just before she graduated they offered her the opportunity to join them covering for one of their assessors who was going on maternity leave. They accepted that she had difficulties with the written word and that she would need to use a computer but said she was one of the best students they had ever trained. What a confidence boost!

After several years Johanne felt she wanted to 'spread her wings' so applied for a job assessing girls working in hotels abroad. Her application was successful and her area was Spain and Majorca. I was worried about her driving about on her own in a foreign country but at the same time I was very proud that she had gained the confidence to deal with such a challenge.

The day she returned to Scotland she spotted a job she decided was for her. It was a project trying to encourage those over 25 to return to work by training them in Child Care. Johanne was still early 20s but again she was successful and excelled in the position.

Johanne missed the 'hands on' with the children. Her early ambition had been to manage a children's nursery so when a job appeared as a Manager in a private nursery she applied and again was successful. The academic route was wrongly blocked but I think Johanne's story proves that even if a different route has to be taken it does not mean that goals cannot be achieved.

Johanne is now happily married with 3 children. Her little boy started school last year. His P1 year had its challenges but at least his teacher, having watched a programme on TV with Kara Tointon, is aware of the indicators of dyslexia. My prayer is that the introduction of the Dyslexia Toolkit and the work of Jackie Stewart and many others plus the willingness of celebrities to tell their stories will mean that teachers are more understanding, more encouraging and more resources are available to ensure all children have school experiences which help them to become confident, well adjusted, successful adults.

Elizabeth Dickson, mother's story of her daughter

76. An old man's magic gift
"it is important for people to see themselves as the "hero" of their own life story"

It was only when my fifteen year old son was diagnosed as suffering from dyslexia that I realised that I too suffered from dyslexia. After all, we were both thought of as being clever but lazy at school. Having left school at the age of sixteen unable to write or spell I should have been able to guess that something was wrong but I had the good fortune (yes good fortune) of going to a lousy school. I say good fortune because, later on when I started on self-education, it allowed me to assume that my learning difficulties were down to the quality of my formal schooling and not that I was stupid as so many dyslexics feel. My part time self-education journey took me over ten years but as the semi-illiterate twenty something grew into a well-educated professional the process was a matter of great personal satisfaction.

One thing I have learned along the way is that it is important for people to see themselves as the "hero" of their own life story, especially if they are to overcome the "dragon" of dyslexia that is barring their way. The knowledge that you are a hero and have the ability to overcome dragon dyslexia is the first gift this old man gives to you.

However, my second gift for you is the magical one, a "light sabre of the brain" as I like to think of it. The gift was given to me by the BBC around 35 years ago and it is the work of Tony Buzan which featured in their "Use Your Head" series at that time. Buzan's work may not be perfect but when struggling with dyslexia we are not looking for perfection we are looking for "a best fit solution" and if anyone has a well-formed better fitting solution I'd dearly like to know about it.

Being dyslexic I tend to think in images rather than words and all my creative thinking is done in images. It is only when I get to the end that I go back and turn it all into words with the help of my trusty spell checker. It is this requirement to use one's whole brain that is at the core of Buzan's work and what makes it such a useful tool when dealing with dyslexia.

So in summary then, the gifts this old man gives you are the knowledge that you are already the hero of your own life story, that you have truly heroic potential, and that you have been shown a magical gift that will help you to achieve your true potential. Good luck on your journey my friends, it will be difficult but you can do it, and, "may the force be with you".
Adult dyslexic

77. Struggling with Dyslexia
"changing jobs all the time meant application forms which always gave me problems."

I have always struggled with reading and writing. When I think back, to when I was a young boy at Primary School - too young I just seemed to get to a stage when it all became a bit too much for me. It wasn't long after that when everything I was given to do was a struggle. I got tired very easily and struggled to concentrate, but I always tried hard to do my best. I remember having a lot of sore heads. Looking back on it now, it was probably because I was always struggling to keep up.

Before high school my mum and Dad went to speak to the Head master at the School about my options. I don't think they were too happy with the results. For the first year I was put in a remedial class, which was meant to give me more help with my reading and writing. After two or three days I realised that the class was full of boys with behaviour problems. At the end of first year I got the chance to repeat first year or stay in the class. I decided to repeat first year in the normal class. Looking back, I wish I'd had the chance of just doing my first year in the normal class. I think

I should have been able to have done that in the first place. I probably would have struggled for a while but would have coped with it if I'd been given a bit of a hand.

At 16, I started my apprenticeship as a bricklayer. I had to do 3 years training. It wasn't the best job but it was work. The job was mainly physical work and didn't involve a lot of writing but when I had to look at plans I always struggled and just like in school I didn't get much help. I hated asking because I felt stupid and just got made a fool of. As an apprentice I would have to go to the shop at lunchtime. I had to write a list. I hated it because I couldn't spell but I had to go. I struggled all through my apprenticeship with my dyslexia.

Eventually the company went bankrupt and I was unemployed. I always found work but the dyslexia was still there. Changing jobs all the time meant application forms which always gave me problems. I had no confidence and always felt stupid, but in the building trade you were always changing jobs.

At last I got a steady job, but working with the local Council meant I had daily time sheets and job sheets to read and fill in. I never liked to have to do this because of my hand writing and spelling, it did not matter how hard I tried my hand writing is very poor.

I often have to use a dictionary or a spellchecker to help me.

Since going to Adult learning, I am beginning to improve, I don't think I will ever be perfect at spelling but I have a lot more confidence. I never treated apprentices or anyone that I work with the same way that I was treated when I was an apprentice because of the way it made me feel.

I don't think you would get away with things like that now and I think there is more help for people like me now.

Adult learner

---

78. Dyslexia is good
"I think it should be renamed the clever people"

It is good being dyslexic. When I first found out I was dyslexic I was 8 years old. Once I found out it was actually good as all the strategies to help me could be put in place, which made everything so much easier.

Before I knew I was dyslexic I thought I was rubbish at lots of things. I then discovered I had Meer Irlens and when I got my glasses it was much better as I could read and copy from the board much easier and I can now catch a ball and track the ball during hockey. I am now going to get Irlens contact lenses so I can play hockey.

I don't understand why they call it dyslexia as I find long words really hard to remember so I think it should be renamed the clever people. I don't do French at school and at first my friends asked me why. I explained that I was dyslexic and that means you can do some things easier than most people like problem solving but it also makes some things harder. I told them that my brain works in a slightly different way than yours. Then no one asked me anymore.

Toe by Toe has made a big difference to my reading and Stareway to Spelling has been great and I am now in the second top spelling group and I was in the bottom before. I think Dyslexia is a good thing. It has lots of good points, it makes me me and I like me.

Pupil, female, 9 years old

79. No longer ashamed of being dyslexic
"the confidence to pursue a career in social care and come out of the closet as a dyslexic"

One of my early memories of school was being humiliated and made to feel like a freak. This was an example of the treatment that that took place at my Primary school when I was 10 years old. We were usually asked to write down what we had done the previous evening or just to write out some spelling words. This I always did to the best of my ability. My teacher would then take the work I had written and announce that she would read out loud my work to the class. Knowing that the work would always be gibberish she always me asked to stand up while she was doing this. She would then make fun of the fact that my work made little sense and was badly spelt. This was excruciatingly embarrassing for me and it would happen with regular occurrence.

When I moved on to secondary school my punishments would be more severe as in those days we were given the belt when any homework was not handed in or work not completed in class. For one and a half years I was given the belt every single day because of tasks I couldn't do or work finish. At the age of twelve and a half I was barely able to write out my full and address. I was labelled by the Scottish Education Department as "stupid".

My family and I moved to London in 1979 where I attended a Secondary School for a few weeks before finding the courage to refuse to go back. I was labelled "disruptive and uncooperative" and because of these labels my case was referred to "The Hackney Home Tuition Centre". It was primarily for young mothers still at school, in fact, I was the only girl that did not have a baby. Thanks to the help and encouragement those teachers gave me I managed to pass three CSE qualifications.

I actively sought out after that, and throughout my adult life, adult education classes to help me improve my reading and writing skills.

I returned to live in Scotland. It was mentioned to me by a friend that I may have dyslexia and should go to the Job Centre. There I was given the name of an educational psychologist. I spent a whole day doing tests and exercises the outcome of which was that I did indeed have dyslexia. He told me that my dyslexia was so severe that he couldn't recommend anything and that "I should accept my fate in life and do manual jobs such as cleaning". This news left me absolutely distraught as I had never been out of work and felt that I could have achieved more in life.

It took me a few years but I eventually got the confidence to contact "Dyslexia Scotland" who supplied me with a list of dyslexia tutors in my area. With the help of a tutor over the next year or so, I learned and tried several different techniques. I found that the "Davis Dyslexia Association" (DDA) programme and Ron Davis' book "The Gift of Dyslexia" worked very well for me. It gave me the confidence to pursue a career in social care and come out of the closet as a dyslexic and no longer be ashamed of it.

I have recently passed my SVQ2 and have a full time job in social care. What could I have achieved if the education system hadn't failed me all those years ago? The Hackney home tuition group were certainly useful but even they didn't spot my dyslexia. There is no point looking back. I have a career that I love and can only go forward into a brighter future.

Adult dyslexic, female

80. Paper, paper, everywhere
"my pile of urgent paperwork just gets bigger."

To get out of bed each morning, I have to negotiate the piles of paper that are stacked beside my bed. There are approximately five or six fairly neat piles. As a dyslexic you would think I would avoid sheets of the written word but actually, I can't seem to get rid of them. I fear that as soon as I throw something out, I will need it. I also find it difficult to file papers in folders and cupboards as I never know what heading to use to file anything.

I am studying part-time, therefore I am reluctant to throw out any papers relating to the course in case they are required as reference material for the next module. As the course is computer based distance learning, I print out the majority of material as I find it very difficult to read documents on a computer screen. Therefore, I have amassed quite a considerable pile of paperwork.

I have also attended lots of Continual Professional Development courses as part of my career development. I have kept all the paperwork from these courses, to refer to them in future. In addition, I come across a lot of work related articles which I print off to read later.

Unfortunately, these articles end up at the bottom of my piles of paper and I never get round to reading them.

Other items that add to my paper mountain are job applications. I keep all the paperwork from every application I submit. The difficulty with submitted applications is that most organisations don't give feedback on their success, so I generally keep the copies for months "just in case". Often this paperwork then ends up under some of the other piles.

Plus there are information leaflets I pick up all the time at work and leisure, often thinking the information they contain will come in handy for future reference. However, these also end up in a pile and eventually the pile becomes unwieldy. When I need to refer to something, I know it is in one of my piles but because of the volume of paperwork, I spend ages looking for it.

Determined to be more organised, I have started a clear out of the piles of paper. But it's so hard to throw anything away! I end up re-organising the pile and only bin a few sheets of paper. I usually come across an article or training session papers I had forgotten I had kept. Despite not having referred to them in months, I decide to keep them as I might just need them.

I also have a paper pile in the kitchen. This is the bills that need paid and bank statements. When I receive a demand for payment I open it and then put it in the pile for action later. About a week later, I will get into a panic when I realise that I haven't paid an account and I may get my electricity, etc, cut off. So I go through the pile, deal with urgent items and leave the rest. Thank goodness for direct debits! I then put the paid bill back into the pile just in case there is a query about it at a later date. Therefore my pile of urgent paperwork just gets bigger.

Then there is my inability to throw out plastic bags – again, just in case I need them in future. But that's another story!

A group of adult dyslexics

---

81. Writing and copying
"I found friends that were happy to write out things for me"

I never knew I was dyslexic until I had a daughter. She was having a lot of difficulty with her speech and letters. When I was at school I used to get my pall to read things out to me we used to get into a lot of trouble for chatting so much. What they never realised was Morag was my eyes. I was able to memorise all the things she read out to me. When we had cooking we always had to copy down the recipe, the teacher would write it on the black board, we would have to read this and collect our flour, sugar, etc. I would have to wait for Morag to read out loud so I could collect what I needed to cook what was on the menu. There was one teacher that noticed I could learn poems much quicker than the rest of the class. He arranged at this point for some of my work to be put on tape recorder so I could listen more. This method was put into place and this made a lot of difference at school. When I was older I found lots of ways to get by, I found friends that were happy to write out things for me. It was my work that became a big nightmare - every thing now has to be recorded as soon as. This was so difficult for me. It was then I started at the abe class and now I am able to write this story to you.

Adult dyslexic

---

82. Problems with balance and writing
"this is part of me and won't let it control me"

I was 35 when I was diagnosed with dyslexia, I was only a screening for dyslexia but it gave me the answers I wanted. When I was younger I had various tests done, I was behind with school work, poor eyesight and hearing loss didn't help. I was told I had coordination difficulties, so all through my youth and adulthood I thought I had coordination problems and struggled through school. When I was in primary school I was behind in maths and always a behind my other class mates. I had poor reading skills, but now my reading has improved and am an avid reader, my creative skills have came through and I now do crafting and have done for nearly 5 years.

My organisational skill are rubbish, I never have anything in the right place, pick up things and don't put them back where they came from My writing and number skills are very bad and have struggled with that all my life thats the worst part of being dyslexic.

My memeory is also bad I don't always remember short term thing like someones name or a joke and concentration is bad I get bored easy and cant concentrate for a long periods of time. I tend to forget to stick to the task in hand. In school I was tought 2 ways of writing at primary joined writing then in high school they thought I would be easier if I printed so this has left me with a mixed way of writing so when I write a passage it has both printed and joined and looks a bit messy this way, only if I concentrate hard can it be easily read but that takes a long time so I tend to not write much and only realy when necessary.

My balance is badly effected but I'm not sure if thats beacase of my hearing problems or the lack of co ordination that comes with dyslexia. My spelling is very bad and find it hard to spell. when I had the co-ordation test I was given some aid to help me in school but it took nearly 3 years to implement anything, it was a small typewriter to help me with school work but technology was rubbish and the tape kept catching on the paper so it was always aways fixed. I was also put into a typing class with a group a year above me to learn to type. I didn't like it much but I think it helped me a little to assit with me school work but I was taken out of cooking and sewing to do this class which I missed.

Over the past few years I found out more about dyslexia and the traits it comes with. I sometimes hate being dyslexic and get frustrated and wish I could be "normal" but I gained the confidence and agnowleged this is part of me and won't let it control me, I will learn to control it and learn new ways of coping.

Adult dyslexic

83. Growing in confidence
"Filling in application forms is difficult"

At school I struggled until I went to High School. I got a lot of help and support there. Being dyslexic has affected my confidence. I worry that people will judge me by my handwriting. I achieved at school and left with decent qualifications but it was still difficult to find a job that I could manage with my dyslexia.

Filling in application forms is difficult. People can be put off by my handwriting but I'm dyslexic, not stupid. My handwriting might be poor but I am a good employee. I do my job well, I'm presentable, I'm honest and a good time keeper but sometimes being dyslexic means I don't get an interview.

I started with Adult Education about 3 years ago to get some help with my driving theory test and I've continued to get help from them with writing and strategies to cope with being dyslexic.

A hard part of being dyslexic is knowing what to tell people and when to tell them. This is getting easier as my confidence is growing and I've been surprised to learn there are lots of people with different levels of dyslexia.

Adult education helps me with my writing and helps with coping strategies that give me confidence.

Adult learner

84. Finally finding myself
"good parenting is essential for preparing children for school and for supporting their learning."

I was born in 1961 and grew up in the Lincolnshire town of Louth at a time when learning disabilities weren't recognised and falling behind in school placed you in a category of being stupid or lazy.

Junior school was a happy experience and, as far as I can remember, my education progressed normally. Secondary school however was an awful experience. Within a month of Y7 I was completely out of my depth, the pace was quicker than junior school and the learning gradient much steeper. I couldn't read fast enough to keep up, by the time I'd finished reading a sentence I'd forgotten what I had read. My spelling was awful as I couldn't recognise phonics to build words. My time management was poor and I couldn't concentrate long enough to organise my thoughts; these factors led to me being in a state of constant anxiety, I would dread going to school.

I remember raising my hand in class to ask for help on a couple of occasions, but explanations were brief and one-to-one support to individual learning styles was non-existent. I began to suffer low self-confidence after I was selected to read aloud in a school assembly. I remember standing on stage looking down at a page of 'cryptic words' and being unable to follow. Minutes felt like hours of humiliation, until finally, I was told to stand aside. The remainder of my school years were spent avoiding the radar of bullies and being told by teachers that I was lazy. My parents couldn't help, as home life hadn't been good, and by the time I turned 16 they had divorced. I didn't wait for my CSE results and have never returned to my school.

When I was diagnosed as dyslexic at 48 it explained why I had always done things the hard way. I quite literally couldn't read instructions, and for many years frustration spilled over into heavy drinking. I was never diagnosed as alcoholic, but it took me several years to give up drinking completely. I've been sober now for almost twenty years. But it wasn't until my dyslexia diagnosis that my life finally made sense. It explained why I'd been unable to articulate my thoughts and ideas, why my sensory skills didn't match my cognitive ability and why I needed to drink to gain confidence.

This sudden realisation came in 2008 after a long battle over my daughter's lack of educational provision. She was born very prematurely, so had difficulty with her working memory. Her junior school let her down; they made no reasonable adjustments for her 11-Plus examination and she was passed over by her non-disabled counterparts. I've spent the following years looking for evidence of how premature birth affects learning. It turns out that ex-premature children do suffer subtle disabilities that may only become apparent in middle childhood, around the time of transfer to secondary school. I have since petitioned the government on this and they're now well aware of these facts: "What the Teacher Needs to Know".

I returned to education to look for answers, to prevent other children from treading our paths. I've since studied GCSEs, A-levels, Neurological Conditions in Children, Health and Social Care and I'm currently working towards an MSc in Child Studies. My daughter is now top set in school. And I finally found myself by helping her.

I know from personal experience that good parenting is essential for preparing children for school and for supporting their learning. My next project is to form a hub of professional service providers to help children and families in our area, to break the cycle of social breakdown and underachievement.

It is high time education set aside its differences and focused on who it matters to most - our children.

I wish to thank those people who have made my journey possible.

Alan Gurbutt, adult dyslexic and father

---

85. Dyslexia is a gift
"people should be proud to have the gift of dyslexia"

I am an eleven year old dyslexic boy and although when I was yonger dyslexia got the better of me I now see it as a gift, the power to see the world in a different dimention. As I do not have a spare, non dyslexic, mind to compare the way I see the world to I cannot describe how someone like me would see things. But I can say that the mind of a dyslexic is an undoughtablly creative one as proven by the almost definitely dyslexic Leonardo da Vinci and Picasso! Albert Einstein was also dyslexic and he was a perfect example of thinking outside the box which is another talent of dyslexic people therefore I believe that for all these reasons people should be proud to have the gift of dyslexia.

Laurence Burns-Mill, 11 year old dyslexic boy

---

86. A lesson for teachers
"Self-confidence is a quality that most dyslexics lack and no wonder"

I became interested in dyslexia in 1969 in my first job, teaching English in a girls' secondary modern school in Cambridgeshire. I was 21 and straight out of university. (In those days you were allowed to teach in England without a teaching qualification.) I remember one girl who handed in a piece of work full of errors. What interested me was that she had spelt the word "fire" several different ways in one short paragraph. How inventive, I thought.

The following year I trained as a teacher. I came north of the border to teach English, first in Edinburgh and then in Fife. I loved teaching English, but was very aware that I did not adequately support the weakest in the class. I took to visiting the Remedial Department on a fairly regular basis. Eventually I invited the head of that department to watch me teach. I remember her first comment: "Do you realise that you have issued about eight instructions one after the other?" My learning began.

I became so interested in what was beginning to be called "Learning Support" that I moved to that specialty and began a series of training courses. But I learnt most from what my pupils and their parents told me and from observing them at work.

I have worked in Support for Learning Departments in both the state and the private sector. Any pupil with specific learning difficulties needs support; though I feel the more robust the support is the better. My ideal was to enable a young person to become as independent of support as possible. Instead I would like them to become competent users of technology, capable of asking for advice and support when they need it, but perceiving themselves as differently enabled. In teaching dyslexic people it seems important both to teach them ways round problems and to work repetitively at the basic skills. I think that learning to touch-type is essential.

There are some wonderfully supportive and imaginative classroom teachers in primary schools and subject teachers in secondary schools. But there are others who seem to work very hard at destroying all the confidence a dyslexic person can muster.

Self-confidence is a quality that most dyslexics lack and no wonder. I remember a girl coming into my room in tears: she was in S3 and a Maths teacher had told her that a child in P2 could answer the question she had just been asked and could not answer. How cruel and how unnecessary! Dyslexics do not need reminding of what they cannot do. They know. From the moment when they discover which reading group they have been put into in P1, dyslexics tend to label themselves as stupid. In fact of course many dyslexics are highly intelligent in ways that will see them having great success after school, but not usually in school. For someone who has to put in a huge amount of effort in reading, writing and organisational skills school days must seem endless.

Persistence is perhaps the quality most needed by people who are dyslexic. They have to work harder to reach the same place as their friends at school; they and their parents have to remind teachers constantly of their dyslexia; they have to work away at all sorts of things that many other people find easy. And this persistence has to continue into adult life.

I am now retired but I remember with pleasure the many lovely people whom I have met through my work – pupils and parents as well as colleagues.

Retired support for learning teacher

---

87. Driven to the depths of despair
"I tried to commit suicide"

From a very early age I always felt left out as I was too slow. My favourite game was hide and seek but counting backwards was difficult to do and I used to count forward instead as it was easier. But I only got laughed at for being different. The anxiety grew worse through primary school. I used to sit in the playground and watch all the other kids play. My anxiety and isolation grew worse and continued into high school because I had the same people in most of my classes. The constant everyday bullying affected my behaviour. I was so frustrated I became aggressive and spent a lot of time at the headmaster's office. I shouted at teachers and began to Miss A Lot of classes to avoid the bullying. I missed a whole year of high school because of getting bullied; it made me not want to go to school.

The relief of leaving school was marred by the bullying I received as I went into the adult world. I tried to look for help but didn't know where to go. When I arrived at the dole office I told them I had a learning difficulty. I thought I was mentally handicapped. They did nothing to help me and put me under a lot more pressure by demanding that I applied for a certain amount of jobs. I felt even more sad and more alone. They were cruel.

My confidence was at an all time low and I was very close to breakdown. I felt sick and humiliated because I couldn't communicate with anyone properly. When I did it felt like they were laughing at me. There was only one way out. I tried to commit suicide. As a result of my admission to hospital I received support and guidance from a team of professionals. This was long overdue. In the end it was my GP and Psychiatrist who said that I did not have mental health issues, I just needed someone to listen. They referred me for dyslexia assessment.

I had three appointments of which one of them was a one to one. The assessment showed that I was indeed dyslexic and my doctor encouraged me to go to college. I didn't feel able to do this because low levels of confidence wouldn't allow me to be comfortable in a crowd. As advised I then went to the job centre and was finally honest with them about dyslexia. It is only now that they have referred me to Adult Basic Education. I've only been at the A.B.E for five weeks now but already I'm beginning to be a more confident person. I'm not hiding from people as much anymore. I'm in touch with people on face book now for the first time in years. I've even stopped smoking!!! I feel healthier and I'm beginning to reveal the real me and not a wall, at last!!
Adult learner

---

88. A mother's efforts to get help
"sometimes it is like hitting your head off a brick wall"

I am writing this on behalf of my son who is 38 years old. It is to say that my son was sent to a Special Needs School when he was younger because of his problem reading and writing. Nowadays things are a lot different and they are kept in main stream schools which is good. My son has a condition called Dysphasia which is speech as well as Dyslexia (which adds to his problem). I have had to push to try and get help for him but sometimes it is like hitting your head off a brick wall - as all these years ago help wasn't readily available. He went to get his eyes tested and wears blue tinted glasses which helps a bit. I also took him to a place in Glasgow which helps Dyslexics which really helped him but it cost me £1000 for nine months treatment which unfortunately I couldn't continue with due to the cost.

After all the negativities my son works with Marks and Spencers and gets on with all the staff and customers. He is very patient with customers and they hold him in high regard with his helpfulness towards them.

Mother of an adult dyslexic

---

89. Determination wins
"A few tears and a moment of rage I pulled myself together"

My dyslexic story ... 27 years ago I was born. I was born me - an individual with dyslexic and with serious determination, a good sense of humour and a fun loving personality. I started school which was the most frustrating thing that had ever happened to me- ah ah ah it drove me mad. I just couldn't get my point across, the more words I struggled with the more people ignored me, the more time I spent in learning support the more people in the play ground bullied me with names(which I couldn't even spell). This hole thing made me so so augury and even more frustrated. I can't tell you much about these times as they where an area of my life where all I could see was concrete walls that frustrated me where ever I went. I went though school after school trying to settle, nothing until I was allowed a reader and scribe and then this unlocked a world of A's and B's grades.

My mother sent me on hundreds of courses with people who "new" the cure (there is no such thing) but they all taut me about how my dylexicness worked and this allowed me to cope. I don't get b's and d's get mixed up, I don't have letters that fly round which I know some dyslexics do. My very own dyslexicness causes me to have no ability to link words and sound and vice versa. I can read in my head but I can't read out loud. I can understand what people say but I can't write it down. Sound is not translated to words. I think in sounds and this makes writing something differcult. It means I can't sing songs very well, I can't speak another language and sometimes I make my own langage up. Overall my dyslexicness is me it made me who I am!

A's and B's allowed me to go to university. Though when I landed these A's and B's I was sceptical about more educations more frustrations. At the back of my head I had those voices of people of the past saying loser, thicko, stupid, this mad me more determind to prove them wrong. So off I went to university where I just had the BEST time of my life. The support was there and no body quested you having it. People where from all parts of life and I just found my balance. Life was for once great. Then to round if off I got a 2.1 and manage to follow my life time dream to be a vet!!!!

Vet school was something else, hard work and once again I started to struggle. They questioned my ability and again my determination kicked in… A few tears and a moment of rage I pulled myself together and off I went. Head down and ploughed my way though. Thank goodness though it seemed to get easier as it came more pratical.

I am now a Vet and I am still dyslexic and I am me.

Young adult dyslexic

90. Dyslexia awareness
"I explained to him that I used the computer because I was dyslexic"

I had no idea about Dyslexia. I asked at work if I could get help with reading and writing. I could read a bit but not too well.

I went to ABE (adult basic education) and found out about dyslexia. They were doing screening tests.

After a while Linda, my manager at work, noticed I was trying things I haven't tried before and I started to talk about it (having dyslexia). Linda was helping me go on to the computer.

One of the directors asked me what I was doing on the computer so I explained to him that I used the computer because I was dyslexic because it helped me to read and complete forms. He asked me questions about Dyslexia which I tried to explain as best I could. From time to time he would ask me how I was getting on.

Now I'm not hiding anything. When I go on courses I say that I'm dyslexic and I get longer to do things. The tutor asked if anything else would help and I asked for my paperwork on coloured paper. The guys at work noticed a bit of a difference.

Adult dyslexic

91. Advantages and disadvantages
"my brain is often too tired to pick up a book."

Dyslexia is the most inhibiting and even distressing handicap. The sufferers do not display any outward signs of the problem that afflicts them; they are just held back from fulfilling their full potential in many areas of activity that others take for granted. Great advances have been made in diagnosing and helping those who suffer from this debilitating handicap and I understand that while there may be no cure the symptoms can be eased.

When I was young in the 20's nobody seemed to understand the problem and it was only many years later I discovered why I read so slowly and writing was such a chore. At the time I was treated as someone who was slow and a possible non-achiever, particularly by my bright and very impatient Mother. Yet I did well at school and was even top of my class in later years but parents did not visit schools in those days; there were no such things as parent-teacher meetings. In retrospect I realised that what I was doing was relying on memory. Unconsciously I was absorbing and retaining a lot more than those who read at normal speed. Even now if I read a book or an article, I can quote back whole chunks of it.

Even now I read very slowly and it is most inhibiting. I do not find time to read all the books I want or even whole of the newspaper, which seems to increase in size every month! In my professional work there are a large number of scripts to read, as well as correspondence with which to deal. By the time I have absorbed all that is necessary in this area my brain is often too tired to pick up a book. I sometimes look at the unread books on my shelf, which I long to delve into, and become quite depressed at how my handicap is holding me back.

The only compensation of being dyslexic is that you are blessed with a better memory than the average person. I made a programme for BBC Radio 4 about memory which I titled "Thanks for the Memory". I interviewed many people who use their memory a lot in their work, as well as academics who had made researches in this area. Many people found the programme interesting but if there was one message that came out of the overall programme, it was that the more we use our memories and exercise our brains, the more we can keep the ageing process at bay.

I have two one person shows I perform around the country and also when entertaining on cruise ships. One in particular is about the life and work of the great nonsense poet, Edward Lear. It runs for one hour and a quarter and there is no room in the story, especially when reciting the nonsense verse to improvise or ad-lib. What amazes me is that I have only to tune into my memory bank and it all comes flooding back. I do not state this with any sense of conceit, it is just a facility I take for granted. Even when writing my memoirs, which were published last year, "Nicholas Parsons, with just a touch of Hesitation, Repetition and Deviation", I never once referred to diaries or scrap books, the information I required to fill 331 pages just came to mind.

In my present professional work the biggest demands made on my memory occur when I am chairing Just A Minute, the comedy show on Radio 4. I have to listen with great concentration to every word spoken by the players and when a challenge occurs, particularly for repetition of a word, know instantly whether it is correct or not, make the decision and move on to keep the pace of the show flowing. If I had any technical back-up, it would become tedious, slow everything down and damage the fun we endeavour to generate. As I said in my memoirs "Aren't I lucky that I have a job which I enjoy and because of the demands it imposes helps to keep me younger than I am!"

Nicholas Parsons, broadcaster, actor

92. Getting help
"don't feel embarrassed and you can get help if you're willing"

I diagnosed with dyslexia when I was 15.

My mum and dad separated when I was 12 year old. I chose to live with my mum.

My mum took a stroke when I was 13, which made me not want to go to school. I didn't go to school much until social work told me I have to go to a children's panel and my dad got custody of me. I had to go to school now. I had missed so much schooling I had to get stuck in but that's easier said than done.

I could not read or write that well so I had to go to learning support classes and I had a reader and a scribe who helped me with my exams. I did okay but I could have done better if I had gone to school.

It was embarrassing being a 13 year old boy who can't read or write on his own.

When I was diagnosed with dyslexia at 15 I did not know what it meant until someone sat down and told me.

Some people thought I was thick because I couldn't read or write on my own but it is not all bad you can get a lot of help and I found out that colours can help people with dyslexia this can be any colour that helps you mind was blue and this helped me a lot. This is called scotopic sensitivity syndrome.

I would tell others who have dyslexia don't feel embarrassed and you can get help if you're willing to and take it step by step.

Learning does not have to be boring you can do any thing you want if you put your mind to it, like instead of writing it draw a picture of what you want to say if you can't spell it so you know what it is.

But now I have the confidence to read and write on my own. This is because I got help when I left school and I still go to English classes for my reading and writing now.

Adult dyslexic, 22 years old

---

93. Alternative help
"I began to go to complementary therapists to learn more about myself."

I was born the fourth in a family which would be seven children. Shy and withdrawn, I had a poor start at school; spending my first year of schooling in a private, one teacher school where I was left to learn to mix. I then went to the big local school with 30 pupils who were all ahead of me in basic 3Rs. Reading to me was some kind of magic when our mother read out to us as home. I simply could not master it. By the time I was 11, I was ashamed of my problem, but no one had discussed it with me or my parents. About this time I met a preacher who taught us a chorus "Read your Bible, pray every day if you want to grow". I realised it was up to me to work at my reading so I started reading the Bible daily and praying.

Soon after, I failed the 11+ because I was so slow at reading the questions. My father was surprised, but he wrote to the Education Authorities saying he thought I was a "late developer" and could I be scored on the part of the paper I managed to finish. The result was I was put into the "A" section in the secondary school as they said I would get more attention there, but if I couldn't cope I would be put in the "C" section as the "B" section was so full. So I was with my friends and took French and Latin, Maths and Science and loved it.

At 15, I was sent to Boarding School. I sat no entrance exam but they simply asked which stream I had been in and so again landed in the "A" section. I cannot understand why they did not question it because I still could not read fluently. However again I was taught in the classroom and could pass exams on that teaching, but I knew I would never go to University because I could not read either for pleasure or study.

On leaving school I went to do Nursing and again we were well taught. I found the drug names hard and the diagnoses, but I worked hard. I became very tired emotionally, physically and mentally. I was determined not to give up. It was then I met the G.P. who became my husband. I managed to complete the training and pass the exam. Then we got married.

A year later my daughter was born, but I was still very tired and had a breakdown when she was five months old. It was all too much. Who has heard of a dyslexic Doctor's wife?!! I spent two months in mental hospital. Years later they discovered I was thyroid deficient.

When I was just under 50 years old, my husband was dying of liver failure due to Hepatitis B. I went to a friend who was training to be a Reflexologist and for the first time in my life I was able to talk to someone about my dyslexia. She suggested I go to a Kinesiologist. I found this so helpful. She explained that because my mother was left-handed and my father right-handed, I had inherited an odd mixture; right brain dominance in sight and left brain dominance in hearing and the two don't work well together for reading. I could understand myself at last! I began to go to complementary therapists to learn more about myself. I discovered that I had a sensitivity to wheat and started on a wheat-free diet. Then I cut out dairy products and after a few weeks my reading improved a little. I also discovered that I was magnesium deficient, and when that was corrected my reading improved again. Hallelujah! If I had had this supplement in my 20s or 30s how different my life would have been. I was miserable a lot of my married life just from mere frustration and lack of fulfilment.

Now I order taped books from Calibre and Listening Books, and I'm trying to catch up on years of not being able to cope with reading material. The bumf that comes through the post, is a daily trial, but I've been so fortunate in all with not having had to go to work. God is good.

Adult dyslexic, 67 years old

94. My story, I am 10 years old
"I am vera good at bilde boats"

It hard to read and spelly if you are dyslexic. At school I wus wurad becuse I needed help to read but now I no I am not slla. After school my mum and dad helps with my homework.

Mum orginis me and I am good with my hands. I am vera good at bilde boats

The Dsc hellps a lot becus we repet owe haps evre day.

10 year old boy

---

95. Coping strategies as an adult
"there are things out there to help."

I was 12 years old and in 2nd year at high school when I was diagnosed by an educational psychologist as initially being dyslexic with numbers. Dyscalculia. I struggle quite severely with numbers and find it impossible to understand bank statements and letters from banks and businesses. I am a Childcare Practitioner. When I was in my early 30s I done a course for my work on Health and Social Care, and discovered I needed support to understand what I was reading I was then told I was Dyslexic with Irlen Syndrome. It has always taken me a lot of time to read and I have to break things down to make sure I can understand things, sometimes I need to double check things with people just so I can be confident in my understanding. I started of working in Administration and always wondered why work was difficult, now I know, it took me years to take my Dyslexia seriously I used to just deny it then after my course I thought perhaps this is something I should try and do something about, a new girl started at my work and we didnt get on initially, then one day we had a meeting. She is a qualified teacher and noticed I was struggling with Dyslexia she herself is Dyslexic and gave me loads of support to get things for me that will help me. Since then I joined Dyslexic Scotland in order that hopefully my husband could understand on ways to help me too as I needed alot of support to help me to deal with our finances.

I am now 34 years old and feel more confident at doing studying knowing there are things out there to help. I was always someone who said I cant do this I cant do that now I say I want to do this im going to do that. When im reading at home I use blue overlays now I know what im reading and I can enjoy a novel where as before it was just words on paper. I still have a really bad memory but now write notes and keep them on the fridge whereas before I didnt have the confidence to do that. I have realised that if I dont keep myself ultra organised and plan well ahead of time I will not be able to do things properly and effeciently which makes me more stressed. I need to keep my stress levels down to a bare minimum or I wont be able to do anything. I need to know what is expected of me at work and infact have now got my work to put all paperwork on blue paper I wear blue tinted glasses at times as I am extemely sensitive to bright light and reading white on black is just to stressful. Someone else puts my timesheets through the computer, I am now looking to change my direction and am doing a home course on beauty therapy. Life can sometimes still be very frustrating but having the confidence to speak up more about Dyslexia is important to educate society and take things at your own pace. I do think businsses and employers need to be more educated about Dyslexia though as I feel there is still not alot of support from these areas.

Carol Reid, adult dyslexic

---

96. No certificate for dyslexia
"It was about fairness"

I use YouTube as my communication coping strategy. I can do most things but it easier for me to use editing software, upload information to a website and communicate via YouTube. It's harder to have to formulate my thoughts, format them and write them down in, say, a letter. Over the years, and spending thousands of pounds on technology, communicating via YouTube is one of my strategies of communicating.

When I was growing up and was really young I was completely different form the other kids. I have memories of being kept back in class, forced to do things and suffering great humiliation, mental and emotional anguish. I can't really explain why because it's in the past and I can only remember the pain and the anguish.

When I was in school my mum wanted to know what was wrong with me. I was 'diagnosed' as being dyslexic, ambidextrous, cross-lateral and stuff. My Mum had issues with my problems but was so pleased at getting her questions finally answered. She was told, "He's an intelligent boy but his writing is crap". I was put into remedial classes at different stages throughout my educational life. I was in a class but it was with different people and not really a suitable environment for me. The dyslexia was never actually dealt with or assisted. The result is that I spent my adult life avoiding, hiding and not admitting dyslexia.

I don't have a 'certificate' to prove that I'm dyslexic and I sometimes even doubt I am dyslexic. The fact that I speak well, have good and bad memory, forget my train of thought, but I don't have any proof so maybe I could just be lazy, lying ... My girlfriend once said I was 'dyslazia' - we all laughed about that. So there are days when I have 'dyslexia' and days when I have 'dyslazia'.

My acceptance of my dyslexia came when I was working on a low budget documentary shoot about dyslexics. We interviewed about 5 or 6 young people who were dyslexic. I stood by doing my bit adjusting lights etc and every one of the youngsters being interviewed talked about their different problems and every one I was saying 'yes, that's me'. It was strange because that was the moment for me. I was about 32 at the time. I'm now 43. I believe it now. Up until then I never believed it. I wonder how life might have been if I hadn't been dyslexic. Would it have been worse or better? I don't know.

A beautiful example of dyslexia for you: I went to doctors. A sign said 'Medical Centre Parking'. I felt I read everything that I needed to know from that sign. Two weeks later I get a letter saying that I had incurred a £120 parking fine. I phoned and asked why? I was told that I should have registered my vehicle when I entered the Centre - which I hadn't done. They referred me to the Car Park signs and asked how I could have missed it. I then wrote a letter to the people asking if they take account of adult learning difficulties. They replied to say that the fine still stood. I wrote back and paid the fine and said I'd be in touch with any consumer show that I knew of to investigate the parking charges. I signed my letter and underneath put 'Dyslexic - yes', 'honest citizen - yes', 'stupid - no'. Two days later I received a cheque refunding the parking ticket. It felt like a major victory. But I spend many hours, twice that much in emotional hours, than what I was being repaid. It was about fairness.

Adult dyslexic

---

97. Getting stressed
"my grany helps me but it dos not help"

I am good at time and mony but I am not good at spelling, verbs, multiplication, division and maths. I like art but I cant Draw and I am good at amagning. I love History it is interesting my class is Lerning adout wwII and some of the people in my old class made fun of me and still do. It has been 1 holl year and I still get Bullead si I try to walk away but thay still follow me. My grany helps me but it dos not help and my Dad maks me sit and do times tables, adding, take away, divison and it makes me get stresst out and go mental. My step Dad dos the same but my mum tells them to stop but thay don't lisin.

Pupil, female, 11 years old

98. Thoughts from an educational psychologist
"Dyslexia is not a minor problem. It is a big one."

Starting from the point that children with dyslexia are at the mercy of the system and the people who surround them, and that these are the things that ultimately hold the keys to the children's progress, here are some thoughts on the matter.

1. Dyslexia Lip Service
In the 1980s it was not uncommon for education providers to believe that dyslexia was a wish pursued by neurotic middle-class parents. Now I come across cases where the word dyslexia is used with little restraint. It is often the case that such lavish use of the word is a prelude to describing a support plan that contains nothing except that the teachers have all been informed that the child has dyslexia. This is irritating, not to say patronising and counter-productive.

2. Confusing Needs and Measures
Confusion exists between educational needs and measures proposed to meet the needs. For example,

"two one-hour sessions of learning support per week" is not a need. It is a measure proposed to meet a need. Similarly, I have often seen under the heading of "Needs" in support plans simply "Dyslexia" or, "He has dyslexia". Dyslexia is not a need. It is something that causes a need. How can suitable teaching approaches be devised if what they are intended to achieve is never said? The solution is to say what the needs are. It isn't difficult.

3. Self-fulfilling prophecies

Failure to progress can more easily be put down to a deficit in an individual rather than to shortcomings in the process which is responsible for their education: "Well, he's got dyslexia – what can you expect?" Now you have a self-fulfilling prophecy. The solution is not to let this happen.

4. The Widening Concept of Dyslexia

Dyslexia is becoming the name for any shortfall in any aspect of a person's literacy. I've seen people said to be dyslexic ranging from fluent readers with marginally less than perfect spelling, to a second year university student, very able and very well educated, who had virtually no literacy skills at all. Yet both, since they were said to have dyslexia, got the same

DSA support. One person I saw had two degrees and the most fluent literacy I'd ever seen but was still said to have dyslexia. Another was severely developmentally delayed, could barely talk and attended a residential special school, but whose primary need was said to be having dyslexia. Yet in no case did the accompanying reports from people who signed themselves as psychologists mention these things. This is not good for these people. Nor is it good for people who have dyslexia. It cheapens their difficulties. It makes highlighting dyslexia that much more difficult and undermines its credibility.

5. Assessment

The problem is the assessment process. It is reliant on the measurement of things that do not exist. It is not known what the tests are actually measuring, let alone what they purport to measure. Nor is it known what the relationship is between these tests and the acquisition of literacy skills. Nevertheless, having measured them with, for example, a four minute test, great significance is placed on the outcome. The write-ups of these, in so far as they are at all comprehensible, look scientific with lots of numbers but are little better than palmistry. We need to get away from this and properly professionalise assessments if we are to strengthen serious acceptance of and support for dyslexia.

6. Intervention

Proposed interventions sometimes part company with common sense. For example, if a person is not very good at sequencing things on a test purporting to be about sequencing things, this is held up as an explanation for why they have not learned to read. Consequently, the way to get them reading is to improve their ability to sequence things. The pattern goes like this:

1. Child cannot read.

2. An adult tests them and finds they are not very good at sequencing things.

3. The adult spends three months training the child to sequence things.

4. The adult retests the child and finds the child can now sequence things.

5. Child still cannot read.

It is unquestioningly assumed that one (sequencing test performance) causes the other (reading skill). There is no consideration that causality might be the other way round, given that reading is possibly the most sequenced thing we'll ever do in life. The child spent three months sequencing things when he could have spent the time adding 40 words to his key sight vocabularies.

7. Self-concept

Often children with dyslexia look at their classmates and are confused as to why they don't seem to have any difficulties. Take two children, sitting next to other each reading the same passage about a historical event. One has dyslexia and the other doesn't. The one who doesn't have dyslexia is doing one thing – learning about history. The one who has dyslexia is doing two things – trying to learn about history and struggling with reading. They begin to think they are not as clever as their classmates. This seeps into every aspect of their learning. Their every experience confirms their fears. It gets them down. They begin to doubt themselves and their abilities more generally. It accumulates over the years and they build, brick by brick, this particular image into their concept of themselves and what they are. Dyslexia is not a minor problem. It is a big one.

Educational psychologist

99. Bullied
"now I know I'm not stupid"

My family life when I was growing up was dysfunctional as my dad was a bully and a taskmaster. He always thought I wasn't trying. My mum was lovely and I was very close to her but sadly my mum died when I was 15 which has left a massive gap in my life.

My school years were not happy years. I was bullied terribly at both primary and high school. I struggled at school. I could never understand things like normal people. I always got embarrassing, low marks but I tried so hard and all my school reports said I worked hard and always put 100% effort in. Socially at school I wasn't good enough to talk to with the cool people. I had 2 good friends at school who in a way felt sorry for me so let me tag along with them. I was horrendously bullied by one girl in particular and her gang who I was absolutely terrified of who took my dinner money off me and my school books when they didn't have theirs, constantly kicked me and pushed as I was changing class and just made my life unbearable and also I was very emotional at school which didn't help as I was called 'Cry Baby'. Some teachers were lovely in particular my maths teacher who I had in 3rd and 4th year in remedial maths.

When I left school the bullying continued at work.

I worked at a factory and one woman who was older than me made it her mission to torment me.

I was married and have a lovely child. I loved my husband although he was manipulative. Then my life took a devastating change emotionally and I had a complete breakdown which has left me struggling with life but I am getting there and the big change is coming to ABE which has helped me so much and given me confidence. ABE suggested I had dyslexia screening and this explained my experience with school and everyday life. Now I know I'm not stupid and wish they had dyslexia screening when I was at school. It would have made a big difference to my life.

Adult dyslexic

---

100. Good coping techniques
"It has helped me develop personal qualities"

I only found out that I was dyslexic a year into my first degree. I wouldn't say that I struggled at school; I just knew that I found it harder than others and as a result had to get my head down and work hard. I now know the issues I had with reading and writing were due to dyslexia and Irlen syndrome. Once I found out, I was frustrated that my schools hadn't picked up on it. Memories of unfinished exams and barely even half read English course books came flooding back. But with further reflection, the development of different coping mechanisms and constant support from my parents has definitely shaped me into the determined person I am today.

I finished my first degree in zoology and have subsequently finished my veterinary degree. Understanding dyslexia and Irlen syndrome has helped develop my different learning strategies and has considerably helped me to achieve my goals – just about to start a career as a vet; a profession I always dreamt of working in, but very few believed I could achieve. The Irlen syndrome was diagnosed after the dyslexia, and I now have tinted glasses that stop the words moving on the page and prevent me getting a headache when reading. These have led me to read for pleasure, something I never before could understand and would never have even considered.

I feel dyslexia is still really misunderstood and it doesn't help when some still believe that it's not real. This can only be rectified through raising awareness and understanding. I don't feel that having dyslexia is a disability. It has helped me develop personal qualities that I feel give me an advantage both personally and professionally.

Young adult dyslexic

101. Support from ABE (Adult Basic Education)
"It wasn't until later on in life that I found real support"

I knew that I was different when I went to primary school and got my first reading book. I couldn't see the words. I was scared of my classmates finding out and making fun of me. It was already nightmare because my mum was a nurse in a hospital for patients with mental health issues and I knew that others in my class would call me names- names like the ones they called the people in the hospital.

I became resentful and frustrated. This led to me always being on the defensive. I became aggressive and nearly got expelled from school. At the age of six, I was assessed by an educational psychologist who gave me a positive diagnosis of dyslexia but I was too young to know whether that was a good thing or bad.

My behaviour improved after this, however, because the teachers were at least aware of my difficulties and gave me a little more time and support.

Unfortunately, when I went to high school, things changed dramatically. I got shoved to the back of the class because I was too slow. I really resented this. It just wasn't right that those who were more able were given much more encouragement than those, like me, who clearly needed help.

When I eventually left school, I was put on a Youth Opportunities programme. It was good in away because I made some friends and had a bit of a laugh, but it taught me nothing.

It wasn't until later on in life that I found real support through going to adult learning classes. My dyslexia has once again been recognised and I know there is always help at hand if I need assistance with personal things like writing a CV or a letter. I've had a long spell out of work but have recently managed to get a job. Unfortunately, the shift work means that I won't be able to keep going to the ABE class now, but I know I can always go back if I need to.

Adult dyslexic

---

102. In the family
"It began to dawn on me that I might have dyslexia too."

I was a smart and creative child, so I don't think I had too much trouble at primary school - though I do remember teachers being impatient with my reading and spelling and my mum being told that I could go to any school that I wanted to – the clear implication being that I didn't try very hard.

I started off in secondary school in the top class and gradually worked my way down to the bottom. Reports always indicated that I could do much better if I only tried harder. I used to get spelling tests home to "help" me and I got particularly told off for spelling the same word in several different ways in the course of one essay. They thought I was lazy. Eventually I came to accept that I was lazy too; that I lacked application.

I scraped through my qualifications with bare passes in everything but art, so I went to art school, where I scraped through a degree course.

It wasn't until my son, a smart and creative child, began to find some aspects of school very challenging, that I started to think about dyslexia – the school thought it unlikely, yet he reversed every number and letter it was possible to reverse and initially found it impossible to read, relying instead on a terrific memory. When I was researching the condition on his behalf, I kept reading about the symptoms and thinking, 'but surely that's normal?' It began to dawn on me that I might have dyslexia too.

My son was eventually diagnosed with dyslexia through educational psychology, after considerable negotiation with the school. Later that year, I paid for an assessment for myself, to find that I was also significantly affected.

The diagnosis had a big impact on me. I felt that part of my childhood had been tainted. I almost had to grieve for the part of me that was never good enough or tried hard enough. The more I learned about dyslexia, the more I saw the links with my patchy lack of self-esteem and poor achievement.

The psychologist who did the test asked me why I wanted to find out, he worried that I would feel bad about myself and that it might not be useful to publicise a diagnosis at work. However knowing that I was smart and that I wasn't lazy gave me confidence and renewed ambition. I started taking Open University courses relevant to my job. I didn't advertise my dyslexia at work but I didn't hide it either; it's not shameful. Eventually my employer sponsored me to complete a degree. With extra time, spell checkers and use of computers – as well as the very helpful format of the OU courses – I graduated this year with a 2:1 in Social Work.

I'm hoping that things will be easier for my son, who is now at university, but I still think that the support is patchy and I worry about the people who are not recognised as dyslexic early enough and are not articulate or confident enough to seek help on their own.

I think it's important to be open about dyslexia – hiding it, pretending it's not prevalent, risks more tainted childhoods, under achievement and low self-esteem.

Say it loud – dyslexic and proud.

Mary Gallagher, adult dyslexic and mother

---

103. Unidentified dyslexia
"I do still have a lot of catching up to do"

The feeling of not being good enough in anything that you were doing at school was not helped by the fact that you were just left out and left behind.

The time that I was at school was 60/70s were I went to school might and might not have something to do with it on the west coast of Scotland. I therefore never went on past 16 to further education. Having virtually no qualifications, scraping a pass in English and a pass Art. I worked in shops as a counter assistant as I could not, apply to work in a bank, my maths was rubbish.

Many years ago my Family moved to the East of Scotland, the only think that I could do was work in a shop as a counter assistant. I really did not want to spent the rest of my life dealing with the public.

The result of this being I managed to find work

that did not involve being in contact with the general public I today still find this hard.

Apart from 8.5 years that I had three children, I was very careful that they did not have the problems at school as I had.

The fact that there has never to date been anyone to say we know what is wrong with you its is not an illness it is just a different way of thinking.

When I was young I did not know how people could read books, which I never really did until I was in my twenties, so I do still have a lot of catching up to do, I love books and can't stop collecting them, most of the time I do pass on to other people.

The thing about being left handed I am very sure has a lot to do with being dyslexic, I have now spoken to many people and they seem to think this too.

Do not ask me to read instructions for things I have to ask someone else in the household to do that I very rarely make sense of them.

One of the biggest hurdles of late is trying to come to grips with texting, which my mum in her 70s managed before me. The next one is to be able to work our PC. Without having to ask fo rhelp I am managing to do this own my own, I have been doing Family tree research lately and hav had to spend quite a bit of time writing bit of history to give the people that went before me, These people were lost to the world, nothing to say that they were here, it is a great pity I did not know about this kind of history yes, I know that there are plenty about Kings & Queens and famous people but not us, good fun and a lot of hard work.

I was on my way back to Scotland from Holiday at the Airport in Sydney I was stopped by the people that do the checks if you are carrying drugs. The lady handed me an A4 sheet that had information which made not much sense to all I could make out was something about Drugs, this is what happens when someone asks you to read in a hurry, if that makes any sense?

The hardest bit of joining the class was going through the door, not knowing what to expect so far this has been a good experience I wish I had done this years ago. It was the teacher at the class that handed me the dyslexia awareness week.

Adult learner

---

104. The first step
"I am looking forward to the future"

At first, I was very frightened to come to the learning centre because when I was younger, I didn't like school. I was always told by the teacher that I was stupid. Therefore, I decided that I wanted to spell and write better.

It was my wife, Irene, who persuaded me to come to the learning centre. One of the tutors gave me a test to do and she found out I was dyslexic. I did not know that when I was at school.

It has been difficult for me to come to terms with my dyslexia.

At first I was angry that I could not spell or write a letter but coming to the centre has helped me. All of the tutors have helped so much in my education. I will always be grateful for their support and understanding not just for me but for all the students. I have also made some friends in the class. It has made me more competent at work and at home it has made a big difference to me. My mother used to say the way to freedom was education. I think she was right. I have made some progress in my study as I now have 2 certificates.

I feel very sorry for people who are dyslexic because I know how it will be hard for them at school and also when they start work.

It is important for them to ask for help from their teachers or parents. Some people cannot read or write – I am very lucky, I can do both.

So always remember that you are not stupid you are different. I am looking forward to the future and so should you in your daily lives.

Adult dyslexic, male

---

105. Dyslexia in the board room
"Everyone knows I have it"

Q: What does Dyslexia mean to you?

"I'm slightly dyslexic. For a lot of people, they think that being dyslexic means that you have a disability. I'm not embarrassed about being dyslexic, in fact other people I know who are dyslexic, like Richard Branson and others are very creative. It takes me slightly longer to do certain things but it's not anything to be ashamed of. I wouldn't want to change anything. It's me."

Q: When did you find out you are dyslexic?

"When my wee boy was tested 8 years ago. He's very creative – he plays piano without reading the music."

Q: How did you feel about being told you were dyslexic?

"I felt something was wrong before I was tested. As over

the years I have struggled with reading, but as I didn't realise I was dyslexic I didn't get any support at school."

Q: What coping strategies have you learned to help you on a day to day basis?

"I take my time. I don't get annoyed in Board meetings for example. Everyone knows I have it. I get on with it. If I'm going on TV, I practise lines, I write them out big and prepare beforehand. I wouldn't read anything on the spot but I would memorise in advance."

Q: What advice would you give to others with dyslexia?

"There are different levels of dyslexia. You have to work out how severe it is for you. Don't be afraid to ask for help and you will benefit from that help."

Q: Do you see dyslexia as a difference or as a disability?

"It is not a disability, it is the way I am, one of the things I have to deal with and I don't let it hold me back. I would certainly employ dyslexic people in my company."

Q: And how does your son feel?

"My son is getting extra support. He is very talented

and creative, gifted and special. If dyslexia is sold as a good thing, it's great. He says 'My Mum's got it so I'm fine too."

Interview with Michelle Mone OBE, co-owner of MJM International and creator of Ultimo lingerie brand.